Long Waves of
Capitalist Development

Long Waves of Capitalist Development

A Marxist Interpretation

Based on the Marshall Lectures given
at the University of Cambridge

Second revised edition

ERNEST MANDEL

VERSO

London • New York

This edition published by Verso 1995
© Ernest Mandel 1995
First edition published by
Cambridge University Press 1980

Verso
UK: 6 Meard Street, London W1V 3HR
USA: 180 Varick Street, New York NY 10014-4606

Verso is the imprint of New Left Books

ISBN 978-1-85984-037-5

British Library Cataloguing in Publication Data
A catalogue record for this book is available from the
British Library

Library of Congress Cataloging-in-Publication Data
Mandel, Ernest.
  Long waves of capitalist development : a Marxist interpretation :
based on the Marshall lectures given at the University of Cambridge
/ Ernest Mandel. — 2nd rev. ed.
    p.   cm.
  Includes bibliographical references and index.
  ISBN 1–85984–037–X.
  1. Business cycles. 2. Capitalism. 3. Marxian economics.
4. Long Waves (Economics). I. Title.
HB3711.M353   1995
338.5′42′01—dc20   95–3101
                                                          CIP

Typeset by M Rules
Printed in Great Britain by Biddles Ltd, Guildford and Kings Lynn

Contents

Preface

This book is an extension and revision of an Alfred Marshall lecture that I was invited to give to the Faculty of Politics and Economics of Cambridge. The subject itself has been fascinating me increasingly since the mid-1960s, when the first signs began to make it obvious that the postwar boom was coming to an end. I have dealt with it already in a chapter in my book *Late Capitalism* (London, 1975). Whereas the concept of long waves in the development of capitalist economy had definitely been out of grace with most Marxists for many decades, it had also received little attention in academic circles. A turn in the real economic situation was necessary before economists again started to pay attention to the long waves, which had been under much closer scrutiny, needless to say, in the period between wars.

By trying to offer a Marxist explanation of the long waves, essentially based on long-term movements in the rate of profit determining, in the last analysis, quicker and slower long-term paces in capital accumulation (of economic growth and of expansion in the world market), I have, I believe, also made a contribution to the debates now increasingly going on among academic economists on the basic reasons why these long waves occur. It will be interesting to see if subsequent attempts to "marginalize" the roles of profits and of capital accumulation, in favor of monetary, psychological, or purely inventive factors, will continue to be the rule among those economists who increasingly turn toward study of long-term movements of economic growth under capitalism. The least one can say is that "practical" capitalists will probably be quicker to agree with Marxist "theoreticians" on that essential point than will many academic economists.

I wish to thank Andre Gunder Frank, David M. Gordon, and Anwar Shaikh for many fruitful and critical remarks made concerning the original manuscript, some of which have had an influence on the final version. But I continue to disagree strongly with the opinions of the first two of these friends, who believe that the long waves can be explained by purely endogenous mechanisms of the capitalist economy.

The first edition of this book was published in 1980. For this edition I have added two chapters which cover both the developing debate on long waves and the further accumulation of evidence concerning their dynamic implications for the present.

EM, April 1994

1

Long Waves: empirical evidence and their explanation through fluctuations in the average rate of profit

Paradoxically, although the theory of long waves in the history of capitalist economy is clearly of Marxist origin (its initiators were Parvus, Kautsky, van Gelderen, and Trotsky[1]), ever since its adoption by academic economists like Kondratieff, Schumpeter, Simiand, and Dupriez, Marxists have resolutely turned their backs on the concept. This has proved to be doubly self-defeating. First, it has made Marxist economists increasingly blind to what now clearly appears to be a key aspect of the industrial cycle: its articulation with long waves and therefore its varying amplitude. Second, it has prevented most Marxists from foreseeing important turning points in recent economic history: that of the late 1940s, which involved a strong upsurge in economic growth in capitalist countries, and the no less striking turning point of the late 1960s and early 1970s, which produced a sharp decline in the average rate of growth of the international capitalist economy.

The existence of these long waves in capitalist development can hardly be denied in the light of overwhelming evidence.[2] All statistical data available clearly indicate that if we take as key indicators the growth of industrial output and the growth of world exports (of the world market), the periods 1826–47, 1848–73, 1874–93, 1894–1913, 1914–39, 1940(48)–1967, and 1968–? are marked by striking fluctuations in these average rates of growth, with ups and downs between successive long waves ranging from 50 to 100 percent.

1

These long waves have been more obvious in the economies of the leading capitalist countries (Britain in the pre-World War I period, the United States in the post-World War I period) and in world industrial output as a whole than in the economies of all individual capitalist countries. The law of uneven development operates here, too. Capitalist countries that are engaged in a maximum effort to catch up with the industrialization process, such as the United States after its Civil War and Japan in the twentieth century, have above-average rates of growth even during the stagnation phase of a long wave. But this fact only underlines more heavily the overall relevance of the long waves.

Let us briefly recall the main statistical evidence we cited for the long waves theory in *Late Capitalism* (Table 1.1).

We would add some statistical material worked out by other authors. Gaston Imbert produced the indexes (based on calculations by Jürgen Kuczynski) of per capita world production (exponential tendencies) shown in Table 1.2. Although some of his chronological arrangements seem arbitrary (reducing the amplitude of the fluctuations), these data confirm the general conclusion of the existence of long waves. It is not difficult to extend these trends by including the strong upsurge of per capita world production during 1948–68 and the subsequent downward trend in the rate of growth.

Imbert added an interesting calculation of long-term trends in world output of energy (Table 1.3). Again, we would strongly disagree with some of the chronological arrangements, but the waves appear no less striking from these figures.

Not long ago, W. W. Rostow published a lengthy book devoted mainly to the problem of the long waves and containing a wealth of statistical data.[3]

Angus Maddison[4] recently presented statistical data confirming the existence of long waves in capitalist development, seven years after we did this in *Late Capitalism*. It is true that his calculations differ somewhat from ours. He tried to verify the existence of long waves for all sixteen OECD countries

Table 1.1. Statistical evidence for long waves theory

	Years	Percent
Annual compound rate of growth in	1820–1840	2.7
world trade (at constant prices)	1840–1870	5.5
	1870–1890	2.2
	1891–1913	3.7
	1914–1937	0.4
	1938–1967	4.8
Annual compound rate of growth of	1827–1847	3.2
industrial output in Britain	1848–1875	4.55[a]
	1876–1893	1.2
	1894–1913	2.2
	1914–1938	2.0
	1939–1967	3.0
Annual compound rate of growth of	1850–1874	4.5[b]
industrial output in Germany	1875–1892	2.5
(after 1945: FRG)	1893–1913	4.3
	1914–1938	2.2
	1939–1967	3.9
Annual compound rate of growth of	1849–1873	5.4
industrial output in the	1874–1893	4.9
United States	1894–1913	5.9
	1914–1938	2.0
	1939–1967	5.2

	Percent for 1947–1966	Percent for 1967–1975
Annual compound growth of industrial output afterWorld War II		
United States	5.0	1.9
Original EEC six	8.9	4.6
Japan	9.6	7.9[c]
Britain	2.9	2.0

[a] Dr. J. J. Van Duijn, *De Lange Golf in de Economie* (Assen, 1979), p. 213, contests this figure. He appears to be right.

[b] R. Devleeshouwer ("Le Consulat et l'Empire, Période de 'takeoff' pour l'économie belge?" in *Revue de l'Histoire Moderne et Contemporaine, XVII,* 1970) gives the following annual compound rates of growth for the Belgian economy: 1858–1873: 6%; 1873–1893: 0.5%; 1893–1913: 4%.

[c] This was down to 7% for the 1967–79 period, and it will continue to slide down. *The Economist* (May 24, 1980) puts the annual rate of growth of Japan's GNP at 4.1% for the 1973–1979 period and estimates that it will decline to 3.5% for the 1979–1985 period.

Table 1.2. Indexes of per capita world production (exponential tendencies)

Years	Percent
1850–1873	2.20
1874–1896	1.40
1897–1913	1.72
1921–1933	–0.49

Source: Imbert, Gaston, *Des mouvements de longue durée Kondratieff*, vol. 3. Aix-en-Provence, Office Universitaire de Polycopie, 1956, p. 27.

Table 1.3. World output of energy (exponential tendencies)

Years	Percent
1850–1873	6.56
1874–1896	4.13
1896–1913	4.80
1921–1933	0.55
1934–1950	2.80

Source: Imbert, Gaston, *Des mouvements de longue durée Kondratieff, vol. 3.* Aix-en-Provence, Office Universitaire de Polycopie, 1956, p. 32.

taken together. This choice seems dubious to us, as the majority of these countries have economies that at least for the period before World War I were not really industrialized and therefore fall outside the realm of the normal business cycle altogether (although of course they were strongly influenced by it).

Also, his periodization differs from ours, as he eliminated the years of World War II, which is unjustified, at least for the United States, and he lumped together the 1870–1913 period into a single wave, thereby eliminating the long depression of 1873–93, an operation in which economic historians certainly will not follow him. Table 1.4 shows his statistical results. However, if we eliminate the nonindustrialized countries from this calculation, we obtain a differentiation between the 1870–90 period and the 1890–1913 period (Table 1.5). And if we correct the chronology to conform to the real historical

4

Table 1.4. Average annual compound growth rates

Years	Percent
1870–1913	2.5
1913–1950	1.9[a]
1950–1970	4.9
1970–1976	3.0

[a] The choice of a 1913–50 period is arbitrary, to say the least. The average underestimates the depressive trend of the 1913–39 period by including the strong upsurge in economic growth in North America starting in 1940. Pekka Korpinen, in his *Theories of Crisis and Long Cycles,* soon to be published by the Economic Research Institute of the Finnish labor movement, uses moving averages for the OECD countries and establishes a clear turning point in 1948–49 (1.13% growth rate in 1948, 5.4% in 1949). This conforms to our estimate. For the United States, the parallel turning point was clearly 1940.

Table 1.5. Average annual compound growth for eight industrial countries

Years	Percent
1870–1890	2.48
1890–1913	3.00

Countries are U.K., U.S.A., Germany, France, Belgium, Japan, Italy, Holland.

movement (i.e., to cover the Great Depression of 1873–93), the difference shifts toward 2.2 to 3.2 percent (i.e., it becomes clearly significant, of the magnitude of 50%). So Maddison's data do not differ essentially from ours, except that they do not go back to the 1826–73 period, which we tried to include in our calculations.

In the meantime, other well-known-economists have also jumped on the long waves bandwagon, among them Professor Jay Forrester.[5]

If we consider the history of capitalist development as a whole, there remain only two important questions regarding the long waves theory. Can it be applied backward to a period preceding 1826, the year of the first modern crisis of overproduction of industrial goods? Can one recognize a long expansionist wave from, say, the French Revolution or the Napoleonic wars until 1826? Can one deduce from the long waves theory that a new expansionist long wave will succeed the present long depression at the end of the 1980s or the beginning of the 1990s? The latter part of Chapter 4 will be devoted to consideration of the second question.

The first question is of interest mainly to economic and social historians. Marx himself doubted that one could properly speak of an industrial cycle before 1826, given the limits of industrialization outside of Britain and the limits of export of industrial goods. Nevertheless, there was a definite quickening of the pace of industrial development between 1790 and the early 1820s and a definite slowing of that pace in the subsequent quarter of a century. It is significant that this same rhythm can be found in the Continental countries that were the most industrialized in that period, Belgium and France.[6]

From the point of view of method, the choice of the key indicators is the first distinctive feature of the Marxist theory of long waves in economic development, as distinguished from the current academic theory. Marxists would refuse to follow those economic historians who center their analysis of the long waves on price and money movements.[7] They would not deny that these movements are relevant to the diagnosis of the long waves, and they would even admit a relative autonomy of monetary phenomena. But they would start from the assumption, essential to Marxist economic analysis, that the basic laws of motion of the capitalist system are those of capital accumulation and that capital accumulation originates in the production of commodities, of value and surplus value, and their subsequent realization. Thus the key indicators of long waves are movements involving output of commodities and sales of commodities. And since Marx considered the world market to be the real framework of economic fluctuations, industrial output and statistics of world exports seem clearly to be the two key indicators. This indicates clearly that Altvater's very mild criticism of our long waves theory according to which we would underestimate the role of relative rates of expansion (and contraction) in the world market is unjustified. Likewise, his remark that large-scale masses of reserve money capital cannot be proved to be in existence at the beginning of an expansive long wave is clearly not true for 1893 (after the long depression there was a plethora of capital in the West that began to be massively exported overseas) or after 1940(48) (the Marshall plan), not to speak of the 1980s and 1990s.[8]

My own contribution to the formulation of a Marxist theory of long waves in capitalist development has been misunderstood. It was interpreted by some critics as a "technological explication" of these long waves.[9] The idea that technological revolutions, of which I discern three following the Industrial Revolution, are the *causes* of long-term upsurges in the average rate of industrial growth does not correspond at all to my analysis.

In reality, any Marxist theory of the long waves of capitalist development can only be an accumulation-of-capital theory or, if one wants to express the same idea in a different form, a *rate-of-profit theory*. It is tautological, from a Marxist point of view, that a sudden long-term upsurge in the average rate of growth of industrial output can only express sudden upturns in the average rates of capital accumulation and profit, inasmuch as we are considering these fluctuations within the framework of the capitalist mode of production. A sudden doubling of the long-term rate of growth of industrial output, coinciding with long-term stagnation of capital accumulation (or, worse, a long-term decline in the average rate of profit), is an absurd hypothesis within the context of Marxist analysis. It is not difficult to demonstrate that it would likewise be absurd from the point of view of classic or neoclassic analysis, nor would it be demonstrable on the basis of empirical evidence.

It is not the purpose of this discussion to refer to the lengthy debate (which has gone on for three-quarters of a century or more) concerning the relevance of Marx's "tendency of the average rate of profit to decline" to the development of international capitalist economy in the nineteenth and twentieth centuries, leaving aside the much more abstract (although by no means uninteresting or unimportant) question of whether that "tendency" can be empirically and historically verified or whether it was intended by Marx only to indicate that it stimulates countertendencies (which are verifiable) but cannot stimulate them forever (the so-called breakdown theory controversy).[10] It is sufficient to indicate that most Marxist economists, as well as many academic economists specialized in industrial or business cycle analysis, generally agree to recognize the fluctuations in the average rate of profit and the average rate of capital accumulation within a 7-year or 10-year industrial cycle. Within each cycle, phases of upturn and prosperity are characterized by upturns in profit expectations and profit realization (profits *ex ante* and *ex post*), followed or accompanied by upturns in the rate of productive capital accumulation.[11] Phases of acute crisis and depression are characterized by declines in the rate of realized profit and profit rate expectations, accompanied by or followed by declines of the rate of productive capital accumulation (i.e., investment).

We shall not go into the nice nuances of these correlations, which are by no means mechanistic, no more for serious Marxist analysts than for serious academic analysts. They take into consideration phenomena of time lags, especially between investment decisions and the final increases in output to which they lead. They take into consideration fluctuations in the amount of money capital available for investment over and above productive capital, that is, the fluctuating division of social capital between productive capital, commodity capital (capital frozen in already produced commodities, i.e., inventories), and money capital, including the phenomena of credit and rates of interest fluctuations. They take into consideration fluctuations in the demand for and supply of money capital, as well as a whole series of subsidiary factors. But the essential movements, those that determine the basic trends of the system, remain the fluctuations in the average rate of productive capital accumulation.

Generally, Marxist economic analysis has considered the movements of the average rate of profit in two different time frames: within the industrial cycle and within the whole life span of the capitalist system (the so-called breakdown theory controversy again).[12] It is our contention that a third time frame must be introduced in order to be consistent both with the overall theoretical analysis and with the empirical data that are available. That third time frame is precisely that of the so-called long waves of 20 to 25 years in duration. They present a real challenge to Marxist economic analysis. Refusal to take up that challenge constitutes ostrichlike denial of reality and implies an admission of theoretical impotence.

It is a challenge to a theory in which the tendency of the average rate of profit to decline plays such an important role to explain how it is possible that following at least three historical turning points in capitalist economic history (after 1848, after 1893, and after 1940 in North America and 1948 in Western Europe and Japan) there were sudden long-term upsurges in the average rate of economic growth. We have already underlined the fact that to have such long-term increases in the growth of industrial output and investment coincide with stagnating or declining rates of profit is theoretically untenable and empirically undemonstrable. So the real problem within the framework of Marxist economic analysis is the following: *Is it possible, with the conceptual tools of Marxist economic analysis, to explain long-term upsurges in the average rate of profit at certain historical turning points, in spite of the cyclic downturn of that same rate of profit at the end of each industrial cycle, and in spite of the secular decline pointing to the historical limit of the capitalist mode of production?* Our answer to this question is a categorical "Yes." We are convinced that what occurred after 1848, after 1893, and after 1940(48) were indeed long-term upsurges in the average rate of profit. And we are convinced that this is perfectly explainable within the framework of Marx's economic analysis, for the following reason.

Several key variables of the Marxist "system" are *partially autonomous variables.* Their correlations are not mechanical. One of the main reasons that there have been so many misunderstandings about Marx's economic theory is precisely that by misunderstanding his method of operating at successively different levels of abstraction (or, if one prefers, his practice of using the method of successive approximation), many of his commentators and critics have attributed to him a mechanical correlation between these basic variables, which is in contradiction not only to the internal logic of his system but also to what he explicitly stated on the subject.

A good illustration in that respect is Marx's theory of wages, which is in opposition to the Malthus-Lassalle concept of the iron law of wages, a theory that can be explained only in the framework of precisely such partially autonomous variables, operating within the inner logic of a coherent system.[13] We cannot here go into a detailed analysis of Marx's theory of wages to substantiate our point. Let us just recall an important consequence of Marx's theory of surplus value. In opposition to Ricardo, he did not see the rate of profit as a linear function of fluctuations in wages. The three main determinants of the rate of profit, for Marx, were the fluctuations in the organic composition of capital, the fluctuations in the rate of surplus value, and the fluctuations in the turnover rate of capital (the rate of surplus value being itself no linear function of the fluctuations in real wages either, as we just mentioned).[14] So, again, what happens to the rate of profit cannot in any way be deduced directly from what happens to real wages. The rate of profit can go up while real wages go up; it can go down while real wages go down. Only by careful examination of all the partially autonomous variables can one arrive at conclusions concerning the current trend of the rate of profit and predictions of its future short-term and medium-term fluctuations.

One might think that this is a digression from our theme. It is not. For by showing how, in Marx's system, there is a complex dialectical interplay of various processes that are not mechanically and one-sidedly predetermined, we understand the method that must be used in order to explain the sudden long-term upsurges in the average rate of profit that alone can explain the sudden long-term upsurges in the average rate of growth of industrial output and world trade after 1848, 1893, and 1940(48), as well as, reciprocally, the long-term decline in the average rate of profit that alone can explain the striking reductions in the pace of economic growth that occurred around 1823, 1873, between the two world wars in the first half of the twentieth century, and at the end of the 1960s.

In other words, a sharp increase in the rate of surplus value, a sharp slowdown in the rate of increase of the organic composition of capital, a sudden quickening in the turnover of capital, or a combination of several or all of these factors can explain a sudden upturn in the average rate of profit. In addition, Marx indicated that among the forces dampening the effects of the tendency of the rate of profit to decline are an increase in the mass of surplus value and a flow of capital into countries (and, we should add, sectors) where the average organic composition of capital is significantly lower than in the basic industrial branches of the industrialized capitalist countries.

Thus one can conclude, at the most abstract theoretical level, that a sudden sharp upturn in the average rate of profit occurs when several or all of the five previously mentioned factors operate in a synchronized way and thereby overcome the previously recognizable long-term decline in the average rate of profit. This does not mean that they cancel the normal cyclical ups and downs of that average rate of profit (i.e., that they eliminate the normal business cycle), but it does mean that they apply a brake to the cyclical declines, which occurs as long as the countervailing forces operate more strongly and in a more synchronized way than before.

Conversely, when these countervailing forces are relatively weak, and when only few (or none) of them operate, the tendency of the average rate of profit to decline will assert itself with full force and will characterize a lengthy period (a depressive long wave) with a low average rate of growth or

11

even a tendency toward stagnation. Again, this does not preclude cyclical upturns in the rates of profit and capital accumulation (i.e., a normal business cycle), but it does explain why the periods of recovery will be relatively weak and short-lived.

Thus expansive long waves are periods in which the forces counteracting the tendency of the average rate of profit to decline operate in a strong and synchronized way. Depressive long waves are periods in which the forces counteracting the tendency of the average rate of profit to decline are fewer, weaker, and decisively less synchronized. Why this occurs at certain turning points can be explained only in the light of concrete historical analysis of a given period of capitalist development leading up to such a turning point.

This analysis must then be completed by an explanation of why a series of factors can remain operative and predominant during a whole historical period, why they are not rapidly neutralized by the very economic results they produce. For example, why does a sharp increase in the rate of growth of industrial output during one cycle not rapidly lead to a situation of full employment and rising difficulties in increasing the rate of surplus value, which will predetermine the next cycle and make it start under much worse profit expectations than the previous one, thereby preventing a cumulatively higher rate of growth during several successive cycles?

Conversely, an above-average increase in the organic composition of capital, a stagnating or even declining rate of surplus value, a pronounced decline in the rate of increase of capital turnover, or a combination of several or all of these factors can explain a long-term decline in the average rate of profit. This analysis must likewise be completed by an explanation of the reasons why such a decline does not automatically produce the results that would make a new upsurge in the rate of profit rapidly possible (e.g., why as a result of a stagnating economy during one cycle there is not such an increase in unemployment that it induces a decline in real wages, which in turn induces a strong upsurge in the rate of surplus value, which can then lead, from the next cycle on, to a strong increase in the average rate of profit, a strong increase in capital accumulation, and therefore a strong increase in the rate of economic growth).

Can empirical evidence for such long waves in the average rate of profit be produced? Data seem to be lacking to achieve that for the industrialized capitalist countries taken as a whole, although much research has been going on for certain periods, and especially for specific branches in specific countries. But these data generally do not cover a sufficiently long time span to be able to shed light on our explanation of the long waves of economic development. In the case of Japan, Christian Sautter has drafted a graph of long-term profitability of Japanese nonagricultural private business for the period 1908–73 that clearly shows the long-term trends (Fig. 1).[15]

However, there is one area in which statistics are abundant and do cover very long stretches of time: that of interest rates. Now, from the point of view of Marxist economic theory, interest rates are by no means parallel to the rate of profit at every given moment. They can exhibit strong divergence from this rate under exceptional circumstances. When a grave economic crisis breaks out, coinciding with a monetary or credit crisis (a "crisis of liquidity" of many capitalist firms and banks), the rate of interest can then shoot up over the rate of profit, as it is a question of industrialists borrowing money not to produce additional profits but rather to save their capital. Conversely, during a deep depression, interest rates can fall far below the average rate of profit, as money capital is abundant and industrial firms retard or stop current investment plans.

But if we look at long-term averages of annual rates of interest, these deviations from the norm are strongly reduced, and one can assume that, at least in their long-term trend, interest rates fluctuate parallel to the average rate of profit. It so happens that a computation of these long-term fluctuations in the rates of interest shows that they correspond in broad outline to the long waves of economic development

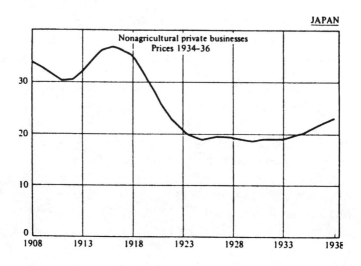

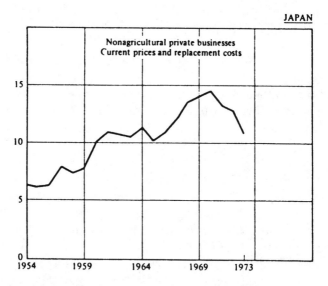

Figure 1. Profitability of Japanese nonagricultural private firms, 1908–1973. Adapted from Sautter.[15]

14

that we have identified. Although this correlation is in itself no definite proof for the Marxist interpretation of the long waves as a function of the fluctuations in the average rate of profit, it certainly strengthens our case.

Long-term interest yields:
    Britain:
        High yield 1798: 5.9%
        Undetermined fluctuations until 1812–1815
        Decline until 1852, then rise until 1874, then new decline until 1897
        Low yield 1897: 2.25%
    United States:
        High yield 1920: 5.32%
        Low yield 1946: 2.19%
        High yield 1974: 7.2% (must be corrected for strong inflation rate; in Switzerland the highest rate recorded was that of 1974: 7.13%)
    France,
        before 1841: declining
        1852–1873: rising
        1873–1896: declining
        1897–1914: rising

Short-term interest rates (decennial averages):
    Britain:
        1805–1845: declining
        1845–1875: rising
        1875–1895: declining
        1895–1925: rising
        1925–1945: declining
        1945–1965: rising
    United States:
        1835–1845: declining
        1845–1855: rising
        1855–1895: declining
        1895–1925: rising

15

1925–1945: declining
1945-1965: rising[16]

Once we have clearly determined the method of approach to a Marxist long waves theory, which is in the last analysis a theory of "long waves in the average rate of profit," we can then stress two other distinctive features of the Marxist theory (as opposed to the academic theory) of long waves in capitalist development, two distinctive features that are closely interrelated.

In the explanation of the sudden upsurges in the average rate of profit after the great turning points of 1848, 1893, and 1940(48), *extraeconomic factors play key roles.* And for the very same reason, Marxists generally should not accept a Kondratieff type of theory of *long cycles* in economic development, in which there is, in the economy itself, a built-in mechanism through which an expansive long cycle of perhaps twenty-five years leads to a stagnating cycle of the same length, which then leads automatically to another expansive long cycle, and so on.[17]

To state it more clearly, although the internal logic of capitalist laws of motion can explain the *cumulative nature of each long wave, once it is initiated,* and although it can also explain the transition from an expansionist long wave to a stagnating long wave, it cannot explain the turn from the latter to the former.[18] There is no symmetry between the unavoidable long-term results of accelerated capitalist economic growth (which is precisely a long-term decline in the average rate of profit) and the sudden long-term upturn in the average rate of profit after a consistent decline for a quarter of a century. This upturn cannot be deduced from the laws of motion of the capitalist mode of production by themselves. It cannot be deduced from the operation of "capital in general." It can be understood only if all the concrete forms of capitalist development in a given environment (all the concrete forms and contradictions of "many capitals") are brought into play.[19] And these imply a whole series of noneconomic

16

factors like wars of conquest, extensions and contractions of the area of capitalist operation, intercapitalist competition, class struggle, revolutions and counterrevolutions, etc. These radical changes in the overall social and geographic environment in which the capitalist mode of production operates in turn detonate, so to speak, radical upheavals in the basic variables of capitalist growth (i.e., they can lead to upheavals in the average rate of profit).

The revolution of 1848 and the discovery of the California gold fields brought about a sudden qualitative broadening of the capitalist world market. Whole areas of Central and Eastern Europe, the Middle East, and the Pacific Ocean were suddenly opened up as markets for capitalist-produced commodities. This tremendous broadening of the market (probably, in proportion, the largest that capitalism has witnessed since its inception) applied a sharp spur to extensive industrialization and to a new technological revolution, as described in detail by Marx in Chapter 13 of Volume I of *Capital*: the passage from the steam machine to the steam motor, from handicraft to industrial production of fixed capital. This, in turn, implied a very strong increase in the rate of growth of productivity of labor (i.e., of relative surplus value, of the rate of surplus value).

Likewise, the rate of turnover of capital increased significantly as a result of revolutions in transportation and telecommunications (the steamship, the telegraph, the increase in railway construction in North America and Western and Central Europe) and revolutions in credit and trade (the joint-stock company, the great department stores, etc.). The combination of all these changes is sufficient to explain a strong, sudden, and durable increase in the rate of profit.

The main features of imperialism (the final carving up of Africa, the Middle East, East Asia, and China into colonial empires or semicolonial spheres of influence, the qualitative growth of capital exports to underdeveloped countries, the decline in the relative prices of raw materials) likewise explain the sudden upsurge in the average rate of profit after 1893 (i.e., the end of the long depression that lasted from 1873 to 1893). A slowdown in the rate of growth of the organic composition of capital, coupled with an increase in the rate of surplus value, again as a result of a technological revolution (electricity), played a key role in increasing in a lasting manner the average rate of profit.

As for the turning point of 1940(48), we have explained at length in *Late Capitalism* the upsurge in the average rate of profit that enabled capitalism to overcome the long relative stagnation it had suffered between 1914 and 1939. Again, the triggering factor was extraeconomic. This time it was neither social revolution (with geographic extension of the sphere of operation of capital, as after 1848) nor imperialist conquest (as in the final part of the nineteenth century). This time the main extraeconomic triggering factor was the historic defeat suffered by the international working class in the 1930s and 1940s (fascism, war, and the Cold War and McCarthy period in North America) that enabled the capitalist class to impose a significant increase in the rate of surplus value (in the cases of Germany, Japan, Italy, France, and Spain, sensational increases ranging from 100% to 300%; in the case of the United States, a more modest but no less significant increase). Accompanied again by a slowdown in the rate of increase of the organic composition of capital (declines in relative prices of raw materials after 1951, easy and near-monopoly access of the United States to cheap Middle East oil, cheapening of many elements of fixed capital since the early 1950s) and by a quickened pace in capital turnover (revolutions in telecommunications and credit, birth of a real international money market accompanying the rise of the multinational corporations), this strong increase in the rate of surplus value is sufficient to explain a sudden upsurge in the average rate of profit, followed by a strong increase in the rate of capital accumulation.[20] The opportunity to invest surplus capital in the armaments sector, with state-guaranteed profits, played a contributing role.

We have said that although the key turning points are

clearly brought about by exogenous extraeconomic factors, they unleash dynamic processes that can then be explained by the inner logic of the capitalist laws of motion. It is at this point that we attribute an important role to *technological revolutions,* as did Marx himself. Our interpretation of the long waves, as compared with those of Kondratieff and Schumpeter, has the advantage that it does not explain the long waves, their origins, and their ends by the doubtful existence of "long-maturing investment projects" twenty-five or even fifty years in duration (which obviously play only a marginal role in the capitalist economy) or, worse, by the sudden appearance of a great number of "innovational personalities" (i.e., by biological or genetic accident), but rather by the long-term ups and downs of the average rate of profit. But once such a long wave gets under way, questions remain: How does it get momentum? Why is it able to sustain itself for a long period? The answers must reside at several levels.

A real technological revolution involves radical overhaul of the basic techniques in all spheres of capitalist production and distribution, including transportation and telecommunications.

Large-scale innovation does not take place during the long wave of relative stagnation that precedes a technological revolution because profit expectations are mediocre. Precisely for that reason, once the sharp upsurge in the rate of profit starts, capital finds a reserve of unapplied or only marginally applied inventions and therefore has the material wherewithal for an upsurge in the rate of technological innovation. When a basic technological revolution occurs, this in itself is already of long duration. Coupled with that material wherewithal is the financial wherewithal, the previous period having witnessed significant increases in newly accumulated capital that were not productively invested (i.e., money capital reserves), which now are added to the strong increases in currently produced and accumulated surplus value to make possible a strong increase in the rate of productive capital accumulation (i.e., productive investment).

19

A real technological revolution means, at least in its first phase, large differences in production costs between those firms that already apply the revolutionary technique and those that do not or do so only marginally. But as the general climate is expansionist, it will be the *average* productivity of labor in advanced branches of industry that will determine the social value of these commodities, and those firms that have above-average productivity of labor will enjoy large surplus profits. The same applies even more for those "new" branches of industry that "carry" the technological revolution. In the beginning, the social value of the commodities will be determined by the firms with the highest production costs. In other words, *technological rents,* under these conditions, drive up the average rate of profit and are not realized at the expense of less productive firms.

Furthermore, the working class generally enters a long expansionist wave bearing the scars of long-term unemployment during the preceding period (reduced bargaining power and, in many cases, shaken self-confidence), so that it will not use the expansionist conditions (at least not immediately) to catch up with the lowering of *relative* wages that had been one of the triggering factors for the upsurge in the rate of profit. Real wages increase, but rather slowly; generally, for at least a decade, if not more, they increase less rapidly than the rate of increase in productivity of labor in department II, which is strongly enhanced by the technological revolution itself. So the rate of surplus value continues to increase, in spite of the rise in real wages.

In addition, the general expansionist climate attracts huge migrations of underemployed labor and impoverished petty commodity producers from the periphery of industrial capitalism to the metropolitan centers. This, in turn, regularly replenishes the industrial reserve army of labor and keeps the growth of real wages within "reasonable" limits from the point of view of the bourgeoisie.[21]

This is certainly the case for the long wave of 1940(48) to the end of the 1960s. Each previous expansionist long wave

20

needs specific analysis in this respect, although there is striking similarity in such migration waves in the 1850s and 1890s.[22]

So all these forces concur to give the expansionist long wave momentum to keep the average rate of growth above average throughout several successive industrial cycles, because the realized and expected average rates of profit remain above the average of the previous long wave.

Certainly this does not mean that the average rate of profit is in continuous upsurge or is more or less level on an above-average high plateau. There is an articulation between the long waves of capitalist development and the normal business cycle. During an expansionist long wave, the periods of upturn, prosperity, and boom last longer and are more pronounced, and the recessions are shorter and less severe. Conversely, during a long wave of stagnating tendency, the periods of upturn and prosperity are shorter, more hesitant, and more uneven, and the recessions last longer and are more pronounced. But during an expansionist long wave there are indeed recessions (i.e., temporary declines in the average rate of profit). Likewise, during a long wave with stagnating tendency, there are periods of upturn and prosperity (i.e., conjunctural upsurges in the average rate of profit).

There is empirical evidence to confirm this articulation. Woytinski gave the following data for two long waves of economic development in Germany: During the depressive long wave of 1874–94 there were fifteen years of crisis or depression, as against six years of upsurge, but during the expansionist long wave of 1895–1913 there were only four years of crisis or depression, as against fifteen years of upsurge.[23] The data presented by Gordon (Table 1.6) permit corroborative analysis for the United States and Britain. These conjunctural ups and downs in the average rate of profit do not need to be explained by the long waves theory. They can be explained perfectly by the traditional theory of crisis (as Marxists say) or business cycle theory (as academic economists call them). But it is precisely the articulation of the

Table 1.6. Articulation between long waves of capitalist development and the normal business cycle

	Ratio of expansion months to contraction months		
	United States[a]	Britain	Germany
Expansionary wave 1848–1873	1.80	2.71	1.61
Depressive wave 1873–1895	0.86	0.76	0.79
Expansionary wave 1895–1913	1.14	1.62	1.33
Depressive wave 1919–1940	0.67	1.36	1.82

[a] Duration of downturn in U.S. for expansionary long wave 1940–1967 was 11 months average; for depressive long wave 1968–1976, 21 months average.
Source: Data are from Gordon, David M., "Up and Down the Long Roller Coaster," in *U.S. Capitalism in Crisis*, New York: Union for Radical Political Economics, 1978, p. 26; Rostow, W. W., *The World Economy, History and Prospects*, Austin: University of Texas Press, 1978, pp. 323, 325, 343. Data for the period after 1967 are from our own computations.

traditional industrial or business cycle with the long wave that makes the long waves theory a useful tool for explaining particularities of each specific industrial cycle and, more concretely, variations in their amplitudes.

When Trotsky correctly rejected Kondratieff's use of the term "long-term cycle" in analogy with the normal industrial cycle, it was essentially because the sudden upward turning points of the long waves cannot be explained primarily by internal economic causes. For that same reason, there can be no mechanical symmetry between the length of the industrial cycle and the length of the long wave. Marxists think (as did Marx himself) that the length of the industrial cycle is dependent on the "moral" life span of fixed capital (i.e., on the distinctive period in which massive renewal of fixed capital occurs), which, by its very physical nature, cannot be renewed piecemeal and on a continuous basis. But such occurrences as new geographic conquests of capitalism, wars, revolutions, and counterrevolutions cannot be commanded by any such mechanical law as the moral life span of large-scale machinery.

However, to deny that once a new long wave is under way the inner logic of capitalism (i.e., the laws of motion of the system) must of necessity command the further trend of events is to deny that these laws of motion are operative in any real sense whatsoever. If one believes that not just once every fifty or sixty years, but continuously, external noneconomic forces determine the development of the capitalist economy, then one rejects out of hand Marx's entire economic analysis.[24]

That is why we cannot accept the criticism addressed to us (and to the Marxist theory of the long waves in general) that we eclectically try to combine exogenous and indigenous explanations of capitalist development (i.e., try to "combine Trotsky and Kondratieff").[25] There is nothing eclectic in the thesis that sudden long-term upsurges in the average rate of profit can be explained, in the last analysis, only through changes in the social environment in which capitalism operates and that once these upsurges have occurred, the inner contradictions of the capitalist mode of production come into their own and inexorably lead to new declines in the rate of profit, both on a conjunctural basis (the industrial cycle) and on a long-term basis. It is inevitable that a new long wave of stagnating trend must succeed a long wave of expansionist trend, unless, of course, one is ready to assume that capital has somehow discovered the trick of eliminating for a quarter of a century (if not for longer) the tendency of the average rate of profit to decline.

In order to illustrate even more precisely this articulation of external and internal factors in the interplay of the long waves of capitalist development and the economic history of capitalism, we must introduce into the analysis of the long waves two additional elements: the long-term trend of international capitalist competition, at state level, and the long-term fluctuations in gold production.

There are indisputable parallels among the relative hegemony of Britain in the world market in the 1848–73 period, followed by the decline of that hegemony in the 1873–93 long depression, the relative hegemony of British imperialism

23

in the 1893–1913 period, followed by the precipitous decline of that hegemony in the 1914–40 period and the strong hegemony of American imperialism in the period from 1940(48) to the late 1960s, followed by the relative decline of that hegemony since then.

It is true that we can speak only of parallels, not absolute identities. The hegemony of British industry in the 1848–73 period was much more pronounced than the hegemony of British imperialism in the 1893–1913 period, which was almost from the start increasingly challenged by the rise of German imperialism and later by the rise of American imperialism. Also, the hegemony of American imperialism in the late 1940s and the 1950s probably outdistances anything the British capitalists witnessed at any time during the nineteenth century. Other differences could be stressed.

But the rhythmic movement is striking in all three cases. We were among the first analysts to announce the relative decline of American imperialism as early as the middle 1960s.[26] There can hardly be any doubt today that those predictions have been completely confirmed by subsequent events.

Under conditions of private property and competition for profit, only a high degree of international concentration of economic and political-military power makes it possible to impose on the capitalist world currently pragmatic solutions in times of crisis, solutions that may or may not help the system overcome its difficulties, but that are imposed nevertheless. When that concentration of power is lacking, when there exist the classic conditions of "unstable equilibrium" among two, three, four, or even greater numbers of capitalist power blocs, then no decisions whatsoever can be imposed, and there occurs a general crisis of international capitalist leadership, which certainly does not help the system overcome its deep depressions more rapidly.

The obvious similarities between the procrastinations of the imperialist powers during and after the 1929–32 depression in regard to efforts to promote any type of international "solution" to the crisis (even stopgap solutions) and the same inability of international capital since 1973 to collaborate (the many "summit conferences" notwithstanding) cannot therefore be considered accidental.[27] Certainly the intensities of international trade wars and protectionist initiatives are less pronounced now than they were in the 1930s. But the reversal of the trend, as compared with what occurred in the middle 1940s, 1950s, and early 1960s, is no less striking.[28] In that period, American imperialism had been able to impose the Bretton Woods system, the Marshall Plan, and the industrial reconstruction of West Germany and Japan without any serious resistance from its competitors-allies, for better or for worse. Today it can do nothing of the sort.

Now, these successive variations in the relationships of forces among the main imperialist (in the nineteenth century, capitalist) powers or power blocs are obviously not to be explained by the "inner laws of motion of the capitalist mode of production" alone, although they are certainly related to the law of concentration and centralization of capital and the law of uneven development. But it is obvious that wars, expansions and contractions of colonial empires or semicolonial spheres of influence, national liberation movements, revolutions, counterrevolutions, and their respective outcomes play decisive roles here. Without the crushing defeat of the German working class in 1933, German imperialism could never have embarked on its course of accelerated expansion and aggression in the 1930s and early 1940s. Without the defeat of German and Japanese imperialism in World War II, American imperialism could never have established the strong hegemony it enjoyed in the 1945–65 period. Without the combination of the decline in British military and political power in World War II and the upsurge in the national liberation movements in Asia and Africa, the collapse of the British Empire could not have occurred in the relatively short time span in which it did occur.

The correlation between fluctuations in gold production and the long waves of capitalist economic development has fascinated many economic historians. After Cassel's pioneering work, many subtle perfections of his basic thesis (to wit, that the long waves are in the last analysis determined by long waves in price movements, in their turn determined by long-term fluctuations in gold production) have been introduced.[29] But from a Marxist point of view, they all suffer from a basic weakness. Gold production in general, or "monetarized" gold output (i.e., that part of current gold production that is bought by central banks, or the rates of increase of central bank total gold stocks, etc.), is always quantitatively compared with total world output and is said to determine the general price trend by means of a relationship between both rates of growth. This is but a crude application of Ricardo's mistaken quantity theory of money applied to gold as money.

Gold can play its role as money (i.e., as general equivalent) precisely because it is a *commodity,* an embodiment of abstract human labor like all other commodities. Therefore, not the quantity of gold produced but the fluctuations of the *value of gold* compared with the average value of commodities will determine the general trend of prices expressed in gold/money, or paper currencies with a fixed "gold basis" (i.e., convertible into a fixed quantity of gold). Thus the key factor to be examined in explaining long-term trends in prices (expressed in gold currencies) is the comparative trend of the productivity of labor in gold mining, on the one hand, and in industry and agriculture, on the other hand.

It has long been understood that gold production fluctuates in a "countercyclic" manner in response to ups and downs in the capitalist economy.[30] But when we seek to determine if this countercyclic functioning is also applicable to the long waves of capitalist development, we have basically to distinguish the situation of nineteenth-century gold production from that of twentieth-century gold output. In the nineteenth century, gold exploration and sudden radical declines in the value of gold caused by the discovery of rich new gold fields were essentially factors of chance. Capital outlays involved in these discoveries were minuscule.[31] It was only after the discovery of the Rand mines in the Transvaal in the late nineteenth century that gold mining became a capitalist industry whose own laws of motion were determined by the logic of capital accumulation.[32] The subsequent development of the Oranje fields, as well as what is going on today after the sensational rise in the "price of gold" to more than $500 per ounce only confirms this rule.[33]

But chance discoveries such as the rich bonanzas of California, Australia, and the Transvaal in the nineteenth century are obviously exogenous factors that cannot be explained (neither in their volume nor in respect to the moment at which they took place[34]) by what occurred during the previous long wave of capitalist development. And by suddenly and strongly depressing the value of gold, they influenced an upward surge in prices that undoubtedly favored an upsurge in the rate of profit; that is, they were among those "environmental" factors that can explain the two turning points in the rate of profit that made possible the two expansive long waves after 1848 and after 1893.[35]

Strangely enough, a Soviet author has followed the opinion of many American and international economists and technocrats concerning the possibility of "demonetizing" gold, defending the idea that "credit money" (bank credit) represents "real money," which can play the same role as gold.[36] This is in contradiction not only of Marx's labor theory of value but also of what has been observed during recent years in the world market: The higher the rates of inflation of the currencies of the leading capitalist countries, the more gold confirms its role as the real measure of the "value" of paper currencies, and the more the rise in the "price" of gold in the world economy will increase. All the schemes for its "demonetization" will fail.

Long Waves, Technological Revolutions, and Class-struggle Cycles

Technological revolutions are impossible without advances in science. To what degree are they *determined* by scientific progress? To what degree can scientific progress be correlated to the development of the productive forces dominated and domesticated by capitalism; that is, to what degree can it be correlated to the inner logic of the capitalist mode of production? It is a fascinating subject whose surface we cannot even scratch in this essay.[1]

A first correlation can be established at the level of the basic historical tendency of capital to transform scientific labor (i.e., "general labor" in the most abstract sense of the word[2]) into a specific form of proletarianized labor (i.e., labor subordinated to the needs of capitalism and controlled by capital). In *Late Capitalism* we pointed out how Marx deduced this tendency from the general laws of motion of capital, thereby describing by anticipation a phenomenon that would not occur in his time but would occur much later. In opposition to a constantly repeated platitude, this confirms that Marx's *Capital*, precisely because of its broad historically anticipatory sweep, is much more a work of the twentieth century than of the nineteenth century:

> In machinery, the appropriation of living labour by capital achieves a direct reality in this respect as well. It is, firstly, the analysis and application of mechanical and chemical laws, arising directly out of science, which enables the machine to perform the same labour as that previously performed by the worker. However, the development of machinery along this path occurs

28

only when large industry has already reached a higher stage, and all sciences have been pressed into the service of capital; and when, secondly, the available machinery itself already provides great capabilities. *Invention then becomes a business, and the application of science to direct production becomes a prospect which determines and solicits it.*[3]

We described in *Late Capitalism* the concrete process by which corporate-dominated research laboratories developed, beginning at the end of the nineteenth century and going through World Wars I and II.[4] However, as Marx predicted, this direct link between scientific progress and the emergence of new technology appears relatively late in the development of the capitalist mode of production. It is preceded by two phases in which capital appropriates in a much more pragmatic way the technical skills of craftsmen-technicians in order to substitute machinery for living labor in the process of constant fragmentation and parcelization of labor for purposes of socioeconomic control over labor (i.e., maximization of the production of surplus labor, which is the driving force of the constantly growing and perfected division of labor within the production process):

1. A phase in which experimentation by craftsmen, occurring in the production process and preceding by centuries systematic experimentation by natural scientists, is directly at the basis of most advances in technology. This phase accounts for most of the period of manufacturing capitalism according to Arthur Clegg.[5] Harry Braverman, following Bernal, pointed out that this also applies to most of the basic inventions of the Industrial Revolution. David Landes made a similar point in *Prometheus Unbound.*[6]

2. A phase in which experimental observation by engineers (or engineers having become capitalists) leads them, as Marx put it, to transform the worker's operations into more and more mechanical ones so that at a certain point a mechanism can step into the worker's place. Here the

contribution of the craftsman to invention might be said to have been largely indirect, although the separation between craftsmen and engineers was not as clear as it sometimes appears from occupational categorizations.

The formal reunification of "abstract science" and "concrete technological inventions" occurs with the appearance of "applied science." It is not possible here to deepen the analysis of the correlation between this appearance and the inner dialectics of the advance of natural science, on the one hand, and the inner logic of the capitalist mode of production (or, better, bourgeois society in general), on the other. This is a subject that merits much more attention from Marxist theorists than it has received up to now. We hope one day to find the time to return to it at greater length.

It must be stressed that the tendency of capital to proletarianize (i.e., subordinate to itself) scientific labor is directly related to the unrelenting thirst for more surplus labor, more surplus value, and more profit, spurred on both by competition and by the class struggle between capital and labor. Therefore it is already interconnected with the rhythmic movement of capital accumulation. It seems obvious that long periods of generally declining rates of profit will tend to encourage research aimed at radical breakthroughs in the field of production cost cutting (i.e., *radical* technological transformations) at the same time as they no less obviously discourage large-scale radical technological innovations; that is, they tend to concentrate current investment on rationalization investment (i.e., investment that is immediately economizing in terms of labor costs).[7] Gerhard Mensch assembled important evidence that clusters of basic innovations occurred in the 1820s, the 1880s, and the 1930s, exactly during stagnating long waves.[8] Economic history, in turn, confirms that the investment outlays for the first massive applications of these basic innovations generally occurred ten years later, after the turn from the depressive long wave to the expansionist long wave had already taken place (Fig. 2).

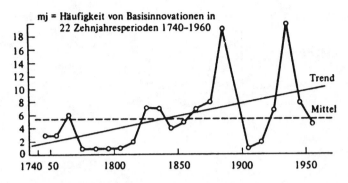

Figure 2. Frequency of basic innovations, 1740 to 1960.

Conversely, when the general atmosphere of bourgeois society is dominated by a buoyant "growth" (prosperity) sentiment, reflecting the sudden sharp real increases in the average rates of profit and of capital accumulation, conditions are more congenial to the huge capital outlays necessary for radical technological revolutions, as opposed to piecemeal current innovations that do not revolutionize basic techniques in all spheres of social life, all branches of industry, transportation, telecommunications, trade and credit, administration, etc. So one can logically conclude that there is rhythmic alternation between intensified research and initial basic innovation (during depressive long waves)[9] and intensified radical innovation (during expansionist long waves). It remains to be determined if the decisive intermediate link (the increase in clusters of inventions) occurs at the final stage of the depressive long wave or if this is too mechanical a correlation between the long-term rhythm of capital accumulation and the long-term rhythm of the "research-invention-innovation cycle" (in case such a correlation is actually proved, the term "cycle" will be justified here).

J. Schmookler has tried to prove that the patent cycle is closely related to the business cycle in general and does not precede or anticipate it.[10] Although the argumentation seems convincing, it does not distinguish between qualitatively different types of patents, and thus it cannot provide an answer

31

to the question we pose. What is decisive is the phenomenon of patents permitting radical innovations, not the patent cycle in general.

W. Rupert Maclaurin[11] introduced distinctions among five successive conditions for innovation:

1. The propensity to develop pure science
2. The propensity to invent
3. The propensity to innovate
4. The propensity to finance innovation
5. The propensity to accept innovation

But although he indicated that "a nation could contribute significantly to pure science and to invention but remain stagnant if too small a proportion of the capital supply in the country were channelled into new development"[12] (here the mediations with profit expectations and the fluctuations of the rate of profit are obvious), he failed to make the distinction between innovations that do not modify the general technique of production and those that do. Combining his analysis with that of Gerhard Mensch, one would more correctly see the following successive conditions for a technological revolution:

1. The propensity to develop pure science
2. A turning point in current inventions leading up to basic inventions capable of changing the whole basic technology of production
3. The propensity to radical innovation
4. Modifications in the general conditions of capital accumulation, profit expectations, and foreseeable market expansions that justify massive outlays for radical innovation[13]
5. The combined effects of implemented radical innovations, rising rates of profit, and accelerated economic growth (capital accumulation) that launch the technological revolution in the real sense of the term.

But at this point in the analysis, a second powerful correlation between the process of capital accumulation and the logic of technological revolutions must be established. Each specific technology, radically different from the previous one, is centered around a specific type of machine system, and this, in turn, presupposes a specific form of organization of the labor process. Let us assume, very broadly, that the successive stages of the Industrial Revolution and of the first, second, and third technological revolutions (always warning against too mechanical an interpretation of these stages and stressing the inevitable existence of transitional forms, corresponding to the law of uneven and combined development) correspond very broadly to the following machine systems: craftsworker-operated (and craftsworker-produced) machines driven by the steam engine; machinist-operated (and industrially produced) machines driven by steam motors; assembly line combined machines tended by semiskilled machine operators and driven by electric motors; continuous-flow production machines integrated into semiautomatic systems made possible by electronics.[14]

It is undeniable that these four successive radically different types of technology and machine systems presuppose four different types of labor organization. The transition from one to another has historically involved serious working-class resistance (among other reasons, because it implies serious deteriorations in working conditions, not necessarily linked to a lowering of real wages or to an increase in the physical work load, but felt and understood by a significant part of the production workers as a deterioration in overall labor conditions). What we want to stress is not so much the consequences as the *origins* of revolutionary transformations in the labor process. In our opinion, they originate from attempts by capital to break down growing obstacles to a further increase in the rate of surplus value during the preceding period. Thereby, again, a direct connection is established with the rhythmic long-term movement of capital accumulation and the increasing (or decreasing) push toward *radical* changes in labor organization. During most of the duration of an expansionary long wave, when the average rate of profit is increasing or staying on a high plateau, the incentive to radically change labor organization (which is tendentiously permanent under capitalism) is less urgent for the bourgeoisie. Huge capital outlays have occurred, and they need to be depreciated and valorized. To replace them too quickly would counteract these needs. Radical changes in labor organization would provoke strong working-class resistance, frequent interruptions of production, and increased class struggle across the board, which conflicts with the normal tendency of the bourgeoisie to try to decrease social tensions when the rate of growth is high and the material means are there to grant some reforms to the working class.

Conversely, toward the end of an expansionist long wave and during a large part of the subsequent depressive long wave, the decline in the rate of profit is pronounced, and that rate remains generally in a trough much lower than during the preceding expansionist long wave. There is then a growing and powerful incentive for capital to radically increase the rate of surplus value, which cannot be achieved simply through increases in the work load, speedups, intensification of the existing labor process, etc., but demands a profound change in that process. Likewise, toward the end of the expansionist long wave, the class struggle generally intensifies for reasons linked to the very long term acceleration of capital accumulation itself (numerical strengthening of the working class, relative decline in unemployment, growing unionization, etc.). Precisely because intensification of the class struggle has already become an objective trend, the hesitation of the capitalist class to further increase social tensions by changing the labor organization will decrease (or, at least, the balance between the divisions inside the capitalist class related to those questions will tend to tilt in favor of those who want to go over to a stronger offensive against the working class).

If we examine the historical stages of introduction of initial machinism, of the first machine systems, of Taylorism, and of continuous-flow labor organization, we can see that although their *experimentation* and initial introduction generally occur toward the end of an expansionist long wave, their *generalization* coincides with a depressive long wave. This is very clear in the case of conveyor-belt labor organization, first introduced in the 1910–14 period,[15] but generalized only after World War I.[16] It is also clear in the case of continuous-flow labor organization, which was limited during the period from 1940(48) to 1968 to a few industries (nuclear power plants, oil refineries, petrochemical plants, semiautomated canneries, bottling and packaging plants in the food industry, etc.); its generalization announces itself only now, through the emergence of microprocessors.

We have, therefore, a striking confirmation, in the field of labor organization, of what we stated earlier in relation to the technological revolutions themselves: There are alternations involving long periods during which they have an innovative character (which pushes up the average rate of profit), followed by long periods during which they take the form of generalization and vulgarization (which pushes down and holds down the average rate of profit).

Furthermore, there is growing evidence that each of these revolutions in labor organization, made possible through successive technological revolutions, grew out of conscious attempts by employers to break down the resistance of the working class to further increases in the rate of exploitation. The first technological revolution was clearly an answer to the struggle of the British workers to shorten the normal workday. Marx himself commented on this at length in *Capital*.[17] The second technological revolution was closely related to the increasing resistance of the strong crafts unions, both in the United States and in Western Europe, to more direct control by management over the work process; in fact, Taylorism arose directly out of the attempts to impose such direct control. Likewise, the third technological revolution had a direct link to the growth of unionization among semiskilled mass-production workers and to the need to whittle away the power of control over conveyor-belt production made possible by union strength of that type. Some authors have suggested that right now attempts are under way toward a new and revolutionary transformation of labor organization as a response of capital to the upsurge in working-class strength and militancy since 1967–8 in Western Europe, the United States, and Japan.[18] And according to studies by historians like Gareth Stedman Jones, one can even apply a similar analysis to the very emergence of the modern factory system, to the Industrial Revolution itself.[19]

Up to this point, all of the processes described seem to correspond in a straightforward manner to the inner needs and logic of capital accumulation, to the objective needs of capital. But at this point, an exogenous element appears. Capital has a constant need to increase the rate of surplus value and to foster deterioration of general working conditions for the working class, and this need is particularly pronounced when it is confronted with a sharp and sustained decline in the rate of profit; but its capacity to realize these ends does not depend on objective conditions alone. It depends also on subjective factors (i.e., the capacity of the working class to mount resistance and counterattack). And this capacity, in turn, is not a straightforward mechanical function of what happened in the previous period: the degree of growth of the wage-earning class, the relative level of unemployment, the level and homogeneity of unionization (more generally, working-class organization) attained.

Although these factors are obviously very important, others must be brought into play: the absolute (numerical) strength of the working class (its weight in the total active population) and of the organized labor movement; the degree of self-confidence and militancy of the working class; its degree of autonomy in relation to predominant bourgeois ideologies; the relative strength of the workers' vanguard inside the class and the labor movement (i.e., the relative strength of that layer of the working class that is qualitatively more independent from bourgeois and petit bourgeois ideology, at least in relation to the immediate central issues of the class struggle); the relationship of forces between that workers' vanguard and the bureaucratic apparatuses dominating the large working-class organizations; the relative strength (or weakness) of an independent anticapitalist pole of attraction inside the labor movement (revolutionary organizations). Added to the subjective factors on the side of the working class there are, of course, subjective factors on the side of the capitalist class (the relative strengths of its different political parties, historical and other factors that favor or hamper recourse to massive restrictions of democratic freedom and massive repression, etc.).

It is the interplay of all these subjective factors with the objective trends outlined previously that will have a decisive bearing on the outcome of the intensified class struggle that generally characterizes most of the depressive long wave. Not only will it decide the length of the interval that must elapse before capital can implement the restructuring necessary to decisively redress the rate of profit, it also will decide the very possibility of that restructuring (i.e., whether the protracted crisis ends with such a restructuring or with a breakthrough toward socialism).

In other words, the emergence of a new expansionist long wave cannot be considered an endogenous (i.e., more or less spontaneous, mechanical, autonomous) result of the preceding depressive long wave, whatever the latter's duration and gravity. Not the laws of motion of capitalism but the results of the class struggle of a whole historical period are deciding this turning point. What we assume here is a *dialectic of the objective and subjective factors of historical development,* in which the subjective factors are characterized by *relative autonomy;* that is, they are not predetermined directly and unavoidably by what occurred previously in regard to the basic trends of capital accumulation, the trends in transformation of technology, or the impact of these trends on the process of labor organization itself.

We assume that there is a long cycle of class struggle (or, to be more precise, a long cycle of rise and decline in working-class militancy and radicalization) that is relatively independent of the long waves of more rapid accumulation and slower accumulation, although to some extent interwoven with them. Without wanting to sketch such a cycle for the entire world proletariat since the inception of the capitalist mode of production, we believe that it is rather obvious for the European working class (Fig. 3).

When we speak about a relatively autonomous long-term cycle of class struggle (strongly determined by the historical effects of cumulative working-class victories and defeats in a series of key countries), we do, of course, mean just that and no more. No Marxist would deny that the subjective factor in history (the class consciousness and political leadership of basic social classes) is in its turn determined by socioeconomic factors. But it is determined in a long-term sense (i.e., within a historical dimension), not by economic developments directly and immediately, nor by those of the immediately preceding period. To give a striking example: Whereas the appearance of massive unemployment weakened the unions' and workers' militancy in the late 1920s and early 1930s in Britain, it had the opposite effect in the 1970s.

It is here that we disagree with the analysis of David Gordon, which in many aspects closely resembles our own. Gordon concluded that resolution of the long-term crisis of accumulation is as endogenous to the system as is the generation of the crisis itself by the previous expansionist long wave.[20] In order to make such a conclusion compatible with the obviously key role that *social forces* (in the last analysis, reducible to the class struggle) play in the outcome of the long-term crisis of accumulation (in the determination of a new sharp upturn in the average rate of profit), he introduced the general concept of "social conditions of accumulation" as predetermining the possibility of the long-term upsurge. At first this appears as a decisive break with "economism," the devil that latter-day Marxists of the Althusser-Poulantzas school relentlessly try to exorcize. But when one gives closer

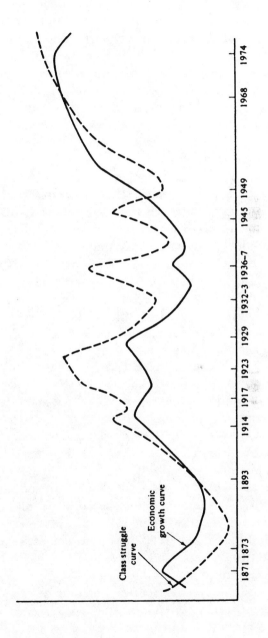

Figure 3. Long waves in European class struggle and long waves in economic growth.

39

attention to the interplay of different factors in the analysis, the striking difference between Gordon's endogenous symmetric long cycles and our asymmetric long waves resides precisely in the fact that we base ourselves on the relative autonomy of the subjective factor and conclude that *the outcome of the depressive long wave is not predetermined* (it depends on the outcome of class struggles between living social forces), whereas Gordon sees the outcome of the depressive long wave as predetermined by the processes of capital accumulation and labor organization in the previous period. "Economism" and straightforward economic determinism are back with a vengeance in the classic tradition of the Second International, all the subtle analysis of institutions, ideologies, decision-making processes, and a host of minor additional factors notwithstanding.

Let us repeat that much of Gordon's analysis is valuable, and it certainly enriches the Marxist approach toward the problem of the long waves of economic development in regard to method and in regard to results.[21] But by trying to discover a single set of unified laws of motion for the functioning of the capitalist mode of production and the changes in its historical and geographic environment, by collapsing into a mechanistic and not a dialectical totality the general and the specific, Gordon inevitably reproduces the weaknesses of all those attempts at explaining long waves that have characterized notably the theories of Kondratieff and Schumpeter. Not by accident, Gordon returns to the "bunched introduction of long-term investment goods" as the basic explanation of the long waves, a working hypothesis that cannot be substantiated after the phasing out of railroad construction as one of the main motors of heavy capital investment. Likewise, it is no accident that the Russian revolution, the Chinese revolution, and the upsurge in national liberation movements in the Southern Hemisphere do not intervene in Gordon's scheme, as they can hardly be considered the outcome of the previous "social structure of accumulation."

What we pointed out with regard to the relatively

autonomous character of the class struggle is likewise true for the rise and decline of hegemonic capitalist powers in the world market and the interference of that movement with basic trends in world market expansion and contraction. To limit ourselves to the twentieth century, neither the October revolution nor the defeat of the German revolution nor the Versailles Treaty nor its collapse nor Hitler's conquest of power can be said to be the logical results of the patterns of capital accumulation or labor organization or the "social structure of accumulation" in the previous long wave of capitalist growth. Although the rise to hegemony of American imperialism has more obvious objective roots, it is sufficient to point out the direct impact that the mass migration of key German scientists to the United States (a result of the *avoidable* conquest of power of Hitler) has had on both the development of nuclear research and the emergence of fully automated techniques closely tied to nuclear power in the United States, to understand how many factors involved in determining the chronology and size of that hegemony were initially undetermined and depended on the outcome and interplay of numerous social, political, and ideological struggles.

Likewise, the rapidity with which the American hegemony has been eroded and undermined (which has surprised many observers who failed to understand the differences between the world of 1945–50 and the world of 1968–78) can in no way be seen as a straightforward function of contradictions in the "social structure of accumulation" that determined the long postwar expansionist wave. They are the combined results of a series of worldwide social and political struggles and their outcomes, something that was absolutely not predetermined when the continuous-flow production process was introduced or when electronics and the multinational corporations came into their own. The real history of the last thirty-five years becomes incomprehensible (or mystified) if we do not take into consideration the fact that political developments and decisions on an international scale are relatively

41

autonomous in regard to the general process of capital accumulation.[22]

The gravest implication of the fatalistic approach of mechanistic economic determinism (an implication *not* present in Gordon's writings, let us state this clearly in order to avoid unnecessary polemics) is that it blurs the polar contradiction of the alternative ways in which a long-term historical crisis of capital accumulation can be resolved. It attributes a kind of limitless power to capital (generally even divorced from concrete social, political, and human forces in which capital *must* be embodied) to attain its historical goals.[23] It thereby offers an excuse and a consolation for all those who bear political responsibility for what occurs in the class struggle and on the world scene. When one says that capitalism can lead either to socialism or to barbarism, one implies that both socialism and barbarism will bear (at least in the initial stage) some of the stigmata of the society from which they arise. But it would be pure sophism to conclude that for that reason it does not really make much difference whether the one or the other triumphs. We might as well say that it makes little difference whether mankind survives or disappears.

For all the indicated reasons, we stick to our concept of a basic asymmetric rhythm in the long waves of capitalist development in which the downturn (the passage from an expansionist long wave into a depressive one) is endogenous, whereas the upturn is not, but rather is dependent on those radical changes in the general historical and geographic environment of the capitalist mode of production that can induce a strong and sustained upturn in the average rate of profit. And although the long cycles of the class struggle and their interrelationship with the search for radical transformation in the process of labor organization must be integrated into that analysis, their relative autonomy must be stressed, as must the decisive role of the subjective factor in determining whether an unavoidable phase of exacerbated class struggle (this phase is, of course, the direct outcome of the long-term crisis in valorization of capital) will end in working-class defeat or victory. The provisional synthesis of all these analytical elements is shown in Table 2.1.

It is interesting to note that in the preparatory investigations of the Systems Dynamics National Project at M.I.T., which are at the basis of the Forrester article, in the unpublished annual report of 1976 of the project to its sponsors, delivered on March 11, 1977, it was said:

> One response to such a condition of excess demand [for capital goods] is to raise the price of capital. Thus in [Fig. 4], high delivery delay in the capital sector leads to increased price of capital equipment. Increased price, in turn, augments the return on investment in the capital sector. Increased profitability of capital-goods production directly encourages more orders for capital, both through expansion of existing capital goods producers and through attraction of new firms to the industry.[24]

Although we would not, of course, agree with the idea that higher profits in the "capital goods sector" (Marxists would say in department I) are caused by higher prices just resulting from increased demand, the strategic role of higher profits inducing higher investment is correctly stressed here. It is a pity that that interesting line of investigation seems to have been abandoned in the further course of the project's labor. The concept of "overproduction of physical capital," handled by Professor Forrester, can never be absolute in a capitalist economy. It is always "overproduction" in relation to potential sales at an expected rate of profit.

The Dutch economist Dr. Van Duijn also made a recent detailed investigation into the long waves problem. He tried to combine Schumpeter's innovation theory with Forrester's concept of demand overshooting for fixed capital goods and added the product life-cycle as a third element of explanation. Now, increased demand in the capital goods sector is induced by increased appearance of new consumer goods, for which additional consumer demand manifests itself.[25] The difficulty with that explanation is that the empirical evidence that Van Duijn himself quoted tends to show that the innovations

Table 2.1. Analysis of long waves rhythm in causal sequence

"Depressive" long wave	"Expansionary" long wave	"Depressive" long wave
Prolonged underinvestment has led to abundance of money capital available		
Accelerated research for new labor-saving and rationalization inventions		
Positive outcome for capital in intensified class struggles previously impeding introduction of new labor processes tied to new techniques		
Strong environmental changes inducing a sudden upturn in the rate of profit (several elements of a b, c, d, and e over a period of time)[a]		
Emergence of hegemonistic capitalist power on world market underwriting relative monetary stability		
	Long-term upsurge in rate of profit and in rate of capital accumulation	
	Massive upsurge of investment allows technological revolution (first phase)	
	Increase in relative rate of surplus value and technological rents give additional spur to rate of profit	

Sustained economic growth favors huge international migration, which enables reproduction of reserve army of labor in spite of increased and heavy accumulation of capital

Spread of new labor processes leads (with time lag) to new forms of resistance and organization of proletariat

Increase in organic composition of capital begins to flatten out rate of profit at relatively high plateau

Strong increase in employment strengthens labor and flattens out increases in the rate of surplus value

Strong demand for raw materials upsets relative price relationship to manufactured goods

Monetary stability shaken by credit explosion necessary to maintain pace of growth in spite of growing contradictions

Intensification of class struggle

Intensification of international competition

World hegemony of given hegemonic power undermined; further erosion of monetary stability overaccumulation

Table 2.1. (cont.)

"Depressive" long wave	"Expansionary" long wave	"Depressive" long wave
	Beginning of long-term decline in rate of profit	
		Attempts to increase the rate of surplus value further sharpen class struggle
		Rationalization investments (second phase of technological revolution, vulgarization of innovations, disappearance of technological rents further saps average rate of profit)
		Monetary instability increases
		Rates of investment and accumulation decline
		Search for new sources of raw materials and new ways to reduce labor costs, but without immediate important results
		Sharpened crisis of capital valorization spreads into prolonged social and political crisis
		Devalorization of capital accentuates

Time sequence →

[a] a, b, c, d, and e refer to the five processes counteracting the decline in the rate of profit indicated on pp. 58–9.

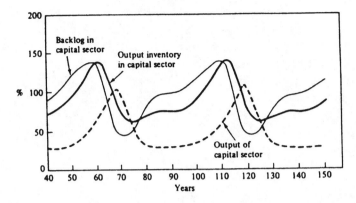

Figure 4. The Kondratieff cycle appearing in the capital goods sector. Adapted from Forrester. [26]

producing the new products generally occur much earlier than the beginning of the new expansionist long wave. Why then the sudden upsurge of capital investment to massively produce them? Again, by leaving out the key factor of a massive increase in the rate of profit, these elements of explanation, valuable in and by themselves, remain insufficient to explain the turning point from the depressive to the expansionist long wave (Van Duijn noted the asymmetry with the turning point from the depressive to the expansionist long wave, which is endogenous). It is closely linked to the phenomenon of over-capacity.

Professor Forrester has made an interesting attempt to build a model leading to an endogenous long wave. It is based on the *supplementary* investment in department I needed to satisfy a big backlog of orders for additional means of production,[26] investment that unavoidably leads to overcapacity. Such a model obviously applies to a wave of radical innovations, i.e., technological revolutions like those described earlier. The weakness of the model (as with so many others) is its elimination of the profit factor, which is the strategic factor for capitalist development. A big backlog of orders cannot present itself to the firms producing machinery and raw

47

materials unless there is a big upsurge in profits and profit expectations. What factors overcome the excess capacity characterizing the depressive long waves? First is the upsurge in the rate of profit, and only after that come the big orders for new equipment. But Forrester's model does not explain the sudden upsurge in the rate of profit. It can only confirm that endogenous factors alone cannot explain the upward turning point of the long waves.

3

Long Waves, Inflation, and the End of the Postwar Boom

We have now to add an additional dimension to the Marxist theory of long waves of capitalist development. The historical turning point of World War I and the turning point of the Russian revolution cannot be eliminated from that theory.

The change in the general environment of the capitalist system, which we used as background or framework for the three successive upsurges in the average rate of profit, the average rate of capital accumulation, and the average rate of economic growth, must be reexamined, amplified, and modified in order to understand that the changes following World War I were of a qualitatively different nature than the changes before World War I.

We shall synthesize these changes in a somewhat provocative way: Revolutionary Marxists contend that with the outbreak of World War I, the historical period of expansion of the capitalist mode of production came to an end. From then on, we entered a new historical period involving both relative decline and geographic contraction of that mode of production. The victory of the Russian revolution and the subsequent losses suffered by the international capitalist system in Eastern Europe, China, Cuba, and Vietnam are significant expressions of that reversal, although by no means its only expressions.

Obviously, these changes are not purely external. Their causes are not basically exogenous. What revolutionary Marxists assert is that capitalism entered a period of protracted structural crisis with the outbreak of World War I, a

49

crisis that can be explained, in the last analysis, by a qualitative sharpening of the inner contradictions of the system (i.e., precisely by the operation of the system's laws of motion). In that sense, the war, the revolutionary upheavals that followed the war, the "secession" of Russia from capitalism, and the exceptional 1929–32 slump only expressed the depth of that structural crisis in a concentrated form. The outcome of these cataclysms is a different matter.

We shall come back to the economic characteristics of that crisis. But before doing that, we want to clarify a question that might seem obscure and unimportant to academic economists, but that certainly is not unimportant for economic historians, historians of economic analysis, and historians of social and political thought in general. This question has also played an important role in discussions among various groups of Marxists. The question is whether or not a structural crisis and historical decline of capitalism excludes new spurts of rapid development in productive forces [i.e., excludes by definition new expansionist long waves like the one between 1940(48) and 1968].[1]

Interestingly enough, the argument has been taken up by two "dogmatic" groups at opposite ends of the spectrum of what we can call Marxist "philosophers of history."

At one end of the spectrum it is contended that because the rapid growth in productive forces and in the international capitalist economy in the first quarter century following World War II is undeniable, the whole notion of an "epoch of capitalist decline" is scientifically untenable and must be thrown out the window.[2] At the other end of the spectrum it is contended that because the decline of capitalism is undeniable (it has, after all, lost one-third of mankind in those areas where it no longer reigns), the development of productive forces after 1940 in North America and after 1948 within the whole of the international capitalist economy is a non-fact (i.e., economic growth, even rapid economic growth, is quite compatible with the concept of stagnation or even decline of productive forces). (We leave aside those who try to escape

50

the real analytical difficulty by denying that capitalism has lost anything and by contending that it still rules in Russia, China, Eastern Europe, Cuba, and Vietnam. Suffice it to say that they could hardly find any capitalist, whether Russian, Chinese, East European, or Vietnamese, to share their bizarre conviction.)

We believe that the concept of a fundamental turning point in the history of capitalism occurring in 1914 is quite relevant from an economic and political point of view. Furthermore, this turning point can be detected at every level of social activity. We believe that the decline of bourgeois society, of capitalist world expansion, of what one could call bourgeois civilization, is an undeniable fact and that its expressions in the economic field can easily be confirmed.[3] One has only to consider the special nature of the economic crisis of 1929–32 to relate it to that decline.

But we also believe that the fact that capitalism entered a period of structural crisis and historical decline in 1914 does not, by itself, preclude new periodic upsurges in productive forces[4] and even a new expansionist long wave like the one we witnessed between 1940(48) and 1968. It only means that the nature of the long wave will be significantly different from the nature of the long wave seen during the period of historical rise and expansion of the capitalist system. We shall examine in what way the specific nature of the 1940(48)–68 long wave of accelerated growth in the international capitalist economy is precisely related to the long-term characteristics of capitalist decline.

Let us take as illustrating the point of our analysis the correlation between the rise and decline of leading capitalist powers in the world market and the rise and decline of the international monetary system. Apparently, there is such a correlation between the rise and decline of the British Empire and the rise and decline of the pound sterling accepted as "world money" (i.e., accepted as being "as good as gold," although the gold reserves of the Bank of England never represented more than an extremely modest fraction of worldwide reserves, 3.6% in 1913). There is an even more striking apparent correlation between the rise and subsequent decline of the absolute hegemony of American imperialism in the international capitalist economy and the rise and decline of the dollar as world money considered as good as gold.

It is interesting to note that the pre-World War I monetary system was not a pure gold standard but rather a *gold exchange standard.*[5] This is not unrelated to a structural characteristic and contradiction in capitalism: the fact that capitalist commodity production tends by its very nature to be world market production, whereas the "many capitals" that organize that commodity production in a competitive way are structured through bourgeois nation-states. Generalized commodity production presupposes (is impossible without) the independent existence of exchange value (money) separate and apart from the currently produced commodities. But money is, in its turn, structured into national currencies. The drive to constantly expand capital accumulation, to constantly increase surplus value realization, combined with the minor (but by no means unimportant) need to economize the use of the special commodity that serves as universal equivalent (gold, or gold and silver, or tomorrow perhaps gold and diamonds), has led to a situation in which gold alone cannot fulfill its role as world money, at least not on a permanent basis. It is only "world money of the last resort." Although there does not exist any bourgeois "world state," and there cannot therefore exist any "world paper money,"[6] paper currencies of specific hegemonic bourgeois states can normally substitute for gold and play the role of world money (i.e., can serve as a means of settling current accounts between firms and nations in the world market and can serve as reserve currencies for other currencies), provided they are precisely "as good as gold."

Even when many paper currencies are tied to gold and the gold standard operates among many countries (final surpluses and deficits in the balance of payments are settled by movements of gold between central banks), current international financial operations are conducted mostly in one or a few national paper currencies. This was the function of the pound sterling in the pre-1914 period.

Likewise, in the framework of the Bretton Woods system, the dollar, being convertible into gold (although not for private American citizens), assumed for all practical purposes the role of substitute world money, this time (the opposite of the pre-1914 system) in large part also serving as reserve fund for central banks, thereby overcoming the strongly uneven distribution of gold among capitalist nations, which was supposed to have been one of the key reasons for the breakdown in international trade after 1929 (already foreshadowed by what happened after the outbreak of World War I).[7]

But it is clear that the specific role of a given national paper currency as substitute world money during a whole historical period cannot be treated as an exogenous factor of the capitalist world economy. Marxists reject out of hand any "political" theory of money in which paper currencies are imposed on unfortunate owner of commodities and promissory notes through the sheer strength of an omnipotent state. Although governments can influence or manipulate the exchange rate of paper currencies, although they obviously can decrease the purchasing power of such paper currencies through massive doses of inflation, they cannot suspend the operations of the law of value, they cannot durably modify relative prices of different commodities, they cannot make buyers prefer more expensive commodities with qualities identical to those of less expensive ones, they cannot in the long run assure larger markets for firms that have lower productivity than for firms that have higher productivity. They especially cannot make capitalists prefer holding liquid or semiliquid balances in paper currencies that lose purchasing power more quickly than others.

When there was a universal demand for more paper dollars amid the ruins of the world of 1945–46, it was not because there was no inflation in the United States (there was already inflation) nor because American tanks, guns, and airplanes were pressuring potential customers into "buying American." It was because American industrial goods were produced under more advanced conditions of technology and productivity of labor than were the goods of other countries, because their quality was generally superior, and especially because the United States was the only capitalist nation that could deliver these goods (i.e., the only nation in possession of huge industrial productive capacity that had not been destroyed or damaged by the war).

If, today, in the imperialist countries, there is a growing run away from the dollar,[8] it is not because there are fewer American tanks, guns, and airplanes than in 1945. Indeed, there are many more, and deadlier ones at that. It is not because the "quantity of money" grows more quickly in the United States than in the other imperialist countries. In fact, it grows less quickly there than in most of them, with the exceptions of Switzerland and West Germany. It is because American industry has become less productive than the industries of many of its key competitors, in a whole series of branches of manufacturing that occupy most of the space of world exports of manufactured goods.[9] It is in lower productivity that the chronic trade balance deficit of the United States finds its basic roots, not in the high cost of imported oil. One could even argue that the decline in the rate of exchange of the dollar as compared with the deutsche mark, the yen, and the Swiss franc (and, with it, the higher rate of inflation in the United States as compared with these countries) is at least in part the consequence rather than the cause of the balance-of-payments deficit of the United States. For under the present international monetary "system" (perhaps one should say non-system) the United States still has, to a certain extent, the possibility of covering its trade deficit by the emission of additional paper dollars, a phenomenon that plays a not unimportant role in fueling the process of inflation in the United States, as well as the rest of the world. This throws constantly growing amounts of devaluating paper dollars into the international circulation and increasingly keeps them there

54

(in liquid or quasi-liquid form, one of the roles of the Euro-dollar and Asia-dollar markets), in strict accordance with Gresham's law. As the supply of these paper dollars is constantly above their "effective demand" in the international money markets, the exchange rate of the dollar is bound to go down in relation to other currencies (at least as long as "all other things remain equal"). There is no way to "stabilize the dollar" within the framework of that existing international monetary "system."

We spoke earlier of *effective* demand for paper dollars, for we can point to an aspect of the world monetary situation that is not so often mentioned, but that confirms, in a negative way, so to speak, the relevance of our analysis. All those countries that have an average productivity of industrial labor substantially below that of the United States are still very eager to buy American manufactured goods. They feel essentially the same urge to obtain and even hoard dollars as did Western Europe and Japan in the immediate post-World War II period. This applies not only to the so-called third-world countries but also to the so-called socialist countries (a wrong definition if there ever was one, but it is not the purpose of these lectures to put it right). Some of them even go to extreme lengths to acquire and hold these devaluated and constantly more devaluating paper dollars.[10] But for precisely the same economic reasons that they are so eager to acquire them, it is very difficult for them to actually put their hands on dollars: They themselves suffer from chronic trade and balance-of-payments deficits with the imperialist countries. In 1976 the forty-five poorest "developing countries" (semi-colonies) had a total trade balance deficit of $10.5 billion. Thirty-five additional non-oil-exporting "developing countries," classified as having a significantly higher income than the first group (annual per capita income oscillating between $400 and $2600, as against $80 to $400 for the first group), suffered a total trade balance deficit of $23.5 billion in the same year (this is a net total, as it takes into account the surpluses of a few countries like the Ivory Coast, Malaysia, Chile, and Argentina in that particular year).[11] The total third-world trade deficit therefore amounted to $34 billion in 1976. As a result of these persistent deficits, the cumulative debt of eighty "developing countries" was $140 billion in 1976 and $244 billion in 1977, and it is estimated that it reached $391 billion at the end of 1979 and more than $1000 billion by the beginning of the 1990s.[12]

So if there is an analogy between the decline of the pound sterling and the decline of British world hegemony, and later between the decline of American imperialist hegemony and the decline of the dollar, the analogy is itself limited and questionable.

The discrepancy between the relative political and military supremacy that the United States still holds in the capitalist world and the decline of the dollar is very striking. Whereas it is possible that that supremacy will be increasingly undermined by a stepping up of Western European and Japanese rearmament, there are many political obstacles on that road, and this will make it at the very least a lengthy process. But even in the whole intermediary period the United States will be unable to stop the erosion of the dollar as a world currency by using its political and military power, although this is still formidable. This erosion cannot be stopped, except at the price of a tremendous depression, graver than the one of 1929–33. And that political price cannot be paid by the United States or the international bourgeoisie, given the current social and political relationships of forces between capital and labor on an international scale.

Here we have arrived at the heart of the question. When the pound sterling was the dominant currency of the world, this was more than just an expression of the supremacy of British capitalism. It was also an expression of a rising, expanding, self-confident, and relatively socially stable capitalist world system. Under these circumstances, the relatively smooth operation of an international monetary system based on gold (and paper currencies convertible into gold, some of which functioned de facto as reserve currencies) expressed both the confidence of the international capitalist class in the capacity of the system to correct its own deviations without heavy interference by governments and the actual capacity of the system to do so.

The crises of overproduction, and the amounts of unemployment they provoked, were not small in the 1893–1913 period. Indeed, some of them were more significant than the 1974–75 recession, at least with regard to the unemployment rates they created.[13] But the relative stability of the system was such that the capitalists thought they could live with such unemployment rates and recessions and overcome them through the normal market mechanisms, without these burdens threatening an immediate political and social collapse of the system. And events showed them to be right, by and large.

After World War I, and especially after the great crisis of 1929–32, the situation radically changed in that respect. Not only was the crisis of 1929–32 the gravest one that the capitalist system ever faced, not only was it an indication of the fact that the inner contradictions of the system had reached explosive dimensions, but also this economic crisis was accompanied by political and social challenges that, after the victory of the October revolution, were incommensurably more dangerous for the system than the pre-1914 ones.

It is in order to avoid or temper the recurrence of massive chronic structural unemployment of the 1929–32 amplitude that all capitalist governments, without a single exception, have adopted inflationary anticrisis techniques. As the French liberal professor Andre Cotta stated so sharply, "We are all keynesians today," including the hardest proponents of "orthodox" monetarist policies.[14] Not a single government, whether right-wing or left-wing, in any capitalist country, applied really deflationary policies in 1975. None came up with a balanced budget, or even a budget surplus, and none applied radical cuts in unemployment compensation (policies that, it should be remembered, were applied during the 1929–32 crisis, and not in unimportant countries).

This choice is not made for ideological reasons, not because Lord Keynes obscured the priorities in the minds of politicians or fooled the public, but for obvious reasons of political and social self-preservation.

It is interesting to note that the "credit inflation" explosion really started with World War I in the United States; that is, it sustained the short-lived boom of the 1920s, was interrupted by the crash of 1929, and came into its own definitely with World War II. (This dovetails nicely with our overall characterization of the post-World War I period as one of structural crisis of capitalism, of the beginning of the decline of that mode of production.) Figure 5 clearly illustrates this.[15]

So the abandonment of the gold standard, the turn toward universal permanent inflation, and the irrevocable decline of paper currencies successively used as reserve currencies under these circumstances are not tied only (or basically) to the decline of American power or American industrial productivity advances. They are tied to the need for capitalism to use inflation in order to try to find solutions, even temporary stopgap solutions, for the increasingly explosive inner contradictions of the system. Without the permanent debt

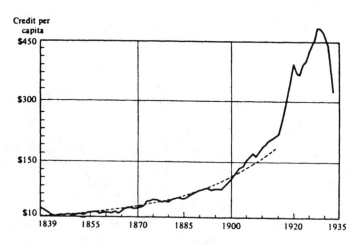

Figure 5. Bank credit per capita in the United States, 1839–1933.

explosion of the last thirty years (public debt explosion during the war, private debt explosion more than public debt explosion in the United States as well as in West Germany and Japan since the war) there never could have been any new long wave of expansion. But that permanent debt explosion is the main root of permanent inflation as a world phenomenon, applicable to the international capitalist economy as a whole. According to Professor Dupriez, exponential growth rates for the 1945(8)–71 period were 1.4 percent for gold reserves, 3.7 percent for currency reserves, and 11.6 percent for credit to the private sector by deposit banks for the ten main imperialist countries.[16] To put it in a nutshell, although capitalism could work itself out of a long period of depression before World War I because of its own inner strength (even after receiving a decisive initial shock from external factors), it could no longer do so after World War I and the great 1929–32 slump. It then needed the artificial stimuli of permanent inflation, growing state intervention, permanent rearmament, etc., in order to embark on a new long-term expansion.

In that sense, whereas the decline of the pound sterling was not rooted in the conditions of its upsurge in the framework of an international monetary system that, by and large, did its job right for capitalism in the pre-World War I system, the decline of the dollar is rooted in the very conditions of its upsurge immediately before and after World War II. It is rooted in the general conditions for capitalist expansion in an epoch of capitalist decline. It is rooted in the very conditions in which the long wave of relative stagnation, 1914–39, was overcome. It reflects, in other words, a basic difference between the expansionist long wave of 1940(48)–68 and the previous expansionist long waves. We have to understand this difference not only to understand the origins of the present depression but also in order to make predictions about the ways and means by which capitalism might overcome that depression in the future. All these considerations clearly indicate the specificity of each long wave in its historical framework, and they must warn against analogies that are too elegant and too mechanical.

In what way was universal inflation since 1940 tied to the explosive inner contradictions of the capitalist mode of production and the means the system used to neutralize, for a quarter of a century, their effects as a decisive brake on economic growth, which they clearly exercised in the 1914–39 period?

In our view (which is by no means shared by all Marxists, but which we can prove is most conforming to Marx's own opinions), the inner contradictions of capitalism (which are the roots of any slow-down or breakdown in expanded reproduction, in capitalist growth) must be found in the sphere of production as well as in the sphere of circulation. Reproduction, as Marx so clearly stated in Volume 2 of *Capital,* is the unity of the process of production and the process of circulation. They are the correlated phenomena of growing difficulties in keeping up the rate of capital accumulation (arising from the tendency of the average rate of profit to decline) and growing difficulties in selling the rising mountain of produced commodities (or, what amounts to the same, fully utilizing the existing capacity of commodity production), given the growing discrepancy between the development of society's productive capacity and the purchasing power of the "final consumers," a discrepancy that is built into the system as a result of all its basic laws of motion.

We cannot here go into a demonstration of why this theory of crises (which transcends the classic opposition between proponents of the crisis-of-overaccumulation theories and proponents of the crisis-of-underconsumption theories) is most conforming to Marx's own writings, most coherent logically, and most able to explain the twenty-two real crises of overproduction that industrial capitalism has witnessed since 1826. Be it sufficient to state that, for us, each crisis of overproduction is simultaneously a crisis of overproduction of capital and a crisis of overproduction of commodities. The exact imbrication of both must, of course, be explained in detail before this thesis will convince anyone. We have not the space here to make this demonstration. We therefore beg the reader's permission to assume it to be proven and to go on from there to study the function of inflation (debt inflation, credit inflation, bank money inflation) in the light of that assumption.[17]

Michel Aglietta has convincingly shown how the concrete mechanisms operate, mechanisms that lead from the monopolies' "administered" prices, through permanent expansion of bank credit and bank money, to permanent inflation of the total money supply, of the "quantity of money," with the complicity of the central banks and the governments. We offered a similar analysis in *Late Capitalism,* and so does Andre Gunder Frank in his book on the current depression.[18] We need not expand on the mechanisms here. It is the tie-in of these phenomena with the overall needs of the system (i.e., their function to temporarily overcome the powerful stagnating trends of declining capitalism, which asserted themselves so strongly in the interwar period) that should be stressed.

Credit inflation has played a dual role in stimulating the long postwar boom. It has created a widely expanded market that in the decisive capitalist country (the United States) accounts for a significant proportion of total sales in two key fields of output: automobiles and houses. A striking expression of this "difficulty of realization" of surplus value, to use the Marxist formula, can be seen in the fact that whereas total private debt accumulated in the United States was 75 percent of the national income in 1945, it reached 100 percent of the national income in 1956 and 150 percent in 1970, and it will be somewhere in the neighborhood of 175 percent for 1980.[19]

Simultaneously, credit inflation has enabled business firms to expand over and above the amounts of surplus value they have appropriated (i.e., to expand by getting deeper and deeper into debt). Here again, some indicators are very striking.[20] And although this tendency has been reduced somewhat by post-1975 recession developments (a big increase in the mass of profits not accompanied by a proportionate increase in investment, so that the debt ratio could be temporarily reduced), it is here to stay as a historical tendency.

To paraphrase a British statesman's famous saying: After World War II, international capitalism floated toward expansion on a sea of debts. Again, this was not an irrational decision of business crooks or demagogic politicians; it was the only way out for capitalism, given the existing economic conditions and social and political relationships of forces.

Business Week has not hesitated to characterize the whole American economy as a debt economy. In fact, at the end of 1978, total American debt had risen to nearly $4 trillion (as against $500 billion in 1946 and $1 trillion in 1960); this growth has been constantly higher than that of the GNP. The annual rate of growth of total private and public debt, which was around 13.5 percent in the 1968–73 period, slowed down during the 1974–75 recession, then reached a new high of 14.2 percent in the 1976–78 recovery. And although the rate of increase of corporate debt was down from 15.6 percent to 12 percent, the rate of increase of consumer debt went up from 12.6 percent to 16.4 percent and that of residential mortgage from 11.5 percent to 14 percent per annum. Total consumer debt at the end of 1978 had reached the staggering sum of $1.2 trillion, thrice the figure for 1969.[21]

This phenomenon is not limited to the United States, although admittedly it is more pronounced there than in other major imperialist countries. Even West Germany, renowned for its conservative monetary policies, saw an upsurge in private debt in the two years 1977 and 1978 from 764 billion DM to 927 billion DM (i.e., 20 percent, a rate of increase that went up to 28 percent during the last quarter of 1978).[22] In the early 1990s total world debt was probably in the neighborhood of $10 trillion (a figure which includes some double accounting), of which only 10 percent was the debt of so-called third-world countries.

Does this mean that it was a "fictitious" or artificial expansion, that the expansionist long wave of 1940(48)–68 cannot, in any way whatsoever, be compared to the classic expansionist long waves of rising capitalism? Of course not.

When the Keynesians, so strongly represented in Cambridge, and the liberal-bourgeois and reformist labor politicians they inspire, proudly point out the achievements of the system during the expansionist wave, they do have an undeniable point. No one can seriously question that there occurred a tremendous leap forward in material production (and not only production of weapons and poisonous or useless goods), that the productivity of labor increased significantly, that the level of employment was significantly higher in the imperialist countries than in the interwar period, that the standard of living of the mass of the population in the West rose in an important way, that many important social reforms that represent real social progress (e.g., the national health service in Britain, generalized paid holidays, and social security systems in most imperialist countries) could therefore be conquered by the workers. And if the mass of the people in semicolonial and colonial countries did not profit from these reforms, one can point out that their existence certainly was not more happy in the 1920s and 1930s, when there was massive unemployment in the West.

So the postwar expansionist long wave is a real wave, not fictitious, if one applies Marxist (i.e., materialist) criteria to judge it: material production, productivity of labor, world exports. There was powerful growth in material production. There was strong expansion in the world market brought about by an upsurge in the average rate of profit and by a subsequent upsurge in capital accumulation. The function of permanent inflation did not consist in bringing about this upsurge (monetary phenomena alone could never achieve that); its function was to bridge over or reduce for a whole period the contradictions inherent in the expansion (i.e., to make it last longer and to postpone the moment of reckoning in which these contradictions would explode in a sharp crisis of profitability and in a sharp crisis of overproduction). In that sense, inflation (i.e., credit inflation) played exactly the same role in the framework of the long wave time span as Marx attributed to credit within the industrial or business cycle:

> If the credit system appears as the main lever of overproduction and overspeculation in trade, this is only so because the process of reproduction, which is flexible by its very nature, is being pushed here to its utmost limits, because a great part of social capital is being used by people who don't own it, and who are therefore ready to act with a recklessness which one doesn't find in a private owner who fearfully keeps pondering the limits of his own property.[23]

When von Hayek and the Vienna school claim "We told you so!" in reference to the inevitable cumulative long-term by-products of permanent "moderate" inflation,[24] they are unable to answer the obvious objection: Their own medicine to over-come the 1929–32 slump failed, and has nowhere produced results. At least the mildly inflationary techniques did overcome it temporarily to produce a quarter of a century of accelerated growth.

How, then, did the next turning point come about? Why was inflation unable to indefinitely bridge over the inner contradictions of the capitalist expansion? What precise economic contradictions determined the end of the expansionist long wave of 1940(48)–73?

In the first place, all through the expansionist long wave one of the basic laws of motion of the capitalist mode of production continued to assert itself. There was a continuous rise in the organic composition of capital.

We are perfectly aware of the fact that this is a subject of great controversy among economists, especially (but not only) non-Marxist economists. We gladly concede that this rise in the organic composition of capital was less pronounced, especially during the first part of the expansionist long wave, than would follow from the very definition of the third technological revolution (i.e., semiautomation). One should not forget that within the framework of Marxist analytical concepts, the purely physical substitution of machines for manpower (which is a general characteristic of capitalist industrialization, especially so in its latest phase, semiautomation) is not a correct indicator of the rising organic composition of capital. This concept concerns value relations (linked to technically predetermined relations), not physical quantities. Furthermore, it concerns not the value of equipment compared with the industrial wage bill (variable capital), but rather the price of equipment currently used, *plus the costs of raw materials and energy,* divided by wages.

Another difficulty consists in the fact that from the point of view of Marxist economic theory, only the wages of productive labor must be taken into account, not the national wage bill. Statistical verification of the rise in the organic composition of capital is therefore impossible on an aggregate basis, starting from the GNP. It is easier to verify on the basis of statistics for industry as a whole, and it is easier yet with separate statistics for each of the main branches of industry.

In *Late Capitalism* we addressed a challenge to our colleagues that has not yet been taken up. Let those who deny the validity of the tendency of the organic composition of capital to rise cite an example of a single branch of industry in which labor costs today constitute a higher proportion of total costs than they did seventy-five, fifty, or forty years ago. It will be difficult to find such an example, not to mention discovering a general trend in that direction. For what is semiautomation all about if not labor-saving-biased technical progress?[25]

Two reports were recently published concerning the future of equipment production in the French telephone and telecommunications industry. Both pointed out that to produce the next generation of telephone exchanges, 50 percent fewer man-hours will be required if the new exchanges are semielectronic and 80 percent fewer man-hours if the new exchanges are totally electronic.[26] Similar figures were recently quoted for the same industry in the United States. Such changes have occurred and are occurring in every single branch of industry, once the third technological revolution is under way. For them not to alter the organic composition of capital would imply either that within a few years the hourly real wage would have to double or quintuple or that with a less rapid rise in wages (of perhaps 50 percent or 100 percent) over the same time period the real costs of raw materials and new equipment would have to decline absolutely by perhaps 25 percent to 40 percent, if one starts from a given proportion of labor costs to total costs at the outset. It is obvious that such assumptions are totally unrealistic and do not correspond to anything that has been going on in any real branch of industry during the last ten to fifteen years, not to mention what is going to happen in the next ten years. To give just one example, consider the semiconductor industry. In the late 1960s the still rather expensive chips could be built by a factory costing $2 million, but $50 million are needed to build a factory for selling today's inexpensive chips at a minimum level of profitability.[27]

Second, as stated earlier, the specific conditions of a *beginning* technological revolution, of the start of new branches of industry, which guarantee huge technological rents (super-profits) for leading firms, slowly peter out when the technological revolution begins to be generalized. Generally, the turn from an expansionist long wave to a stagnating long wave is coupled, in the history of capitalism, with such turns from revolutionary introduction to general vulgarization of new techniques. Technological rents begin to become scarce. Prices of typical "new" products begin to fall under the impact of massive output and a return to competition.

The computer industry is an excellent example of that trend. The evolution from the vacuum-tube-based computer to the transistor computer and then to silicon-based integrated circuits has reduced costs on a tremendous scale, notably in function of mass production. Between 1965 and 1971, costs declined to such an extent that the average price per circuit function (one transistor) fell from $2 to less than 3 cents. In

Germany, the price collapse was even more pronounced (from around 2 DM for a transistor in 1965 to 0.002 DM per transistor function in an integrated circuit today). All the functions of the first American computer (ENIAC, which cost $2 million in 1943) can be performed today by microcomputers that cost no more than $50 to $500.[28]

As a result of this vulgarization of the third technological revolution through microprocessors,[29] the monopoly of IBM in the computer field and the huge technological rents it receives on that basis are doubly threatened, on the one hand by rising American competitors who gained a lead in the microprocessor field (e.g., Texas Instruments, Control Data, Honeywell-Bull, Burroughs, Intel, and Amdahl) and on the other hand by a combined offensive from the Japanese monopoly Fujitsu and the German multinational Siemens, in close collaboration with each other, who are preparing to beat IBM on its own field (i.e., the next generation of large computers).[30] Whether or not they will succeed remains to be seen, but that this will lead to an erosion of monopoly surplus profits through severe price competition seems certain. In the United States, Wall Street has already anticipated such an erosion, for the price/earning ratio of IBM stocks has gone down from 30/1 in the 1960s to 13/1 today. It is calculated that in West Germany average computer prices declined absolutely by 11.5 percent between 1971 and 1977 and that the relative decline (taking into consideration the rise in prices of manufactured goods in general) was as much as 54.9 percent.[31]

With the decline of these huge technological rents, the average mass of profit is doubly threatened. Now it is no longer the firm with the lowest productivity that determines the value of these "innovation" products, given that its production and marketing conditions have become "normalized," that conditions of structural scarcity have disappeared. Insofar as positions of relative monopoly still exist and surplus profits are still realized, they are now increasingly realized at the expense of less productive firms (i.e., they no longer increase the total mass of profits). One can also speak of a beginning decline in the rate of innovation and of a stagnation of revolutionary "information" (cybernetic) expenditure as part of per capita national income starting with 1965.[32]

Many reasons can be given for this decline in the rate and impact of innovations. Many sources attest to it. To quote *The Economist* on the chemical industry:

> Technology has reached a plateau. The pioneering days of knitting new molecular combinations for big new plastics and fibers are over. Only the more difficult molecular chains are left to be worked on, and the promise of high returns has faded. There is no imminent successor to the faded petrochemical boom, though dearer oil and gas are bringing forward the day when making chemicals from vegetable raw materials becomes profitable. The industry is beginning to think about applications of biochemical and genetic techniques. But early results from, for example, synthetic proteins and drug-from-bugs (that is, using natural rather than synthetic chemistry) are disappointing. It will take 10–20 years before any big new stimulus from this quarter transforms the industry.[33]

This is neither only nor basically a question of lack of scientific knowledge, of lack of inventions. It is a question of profitability, as *The Economist* correctly stressed, and a question of general socioeconomic climate in respect to both future market and future profit expectations. In order for innovation to follow invention, important reductions in costs (gains in productivity) must be accompanied by the possibility of mass production (i.e., rapid diffusion of the innovating commodities). Therefore, technical progress can appear to slow down when the passage from invention to innovation becomes more difficult (i.e., less profitable) and when the diffusion of radically new techniques and radically new products becomes more hazardous, as a result of the general slowdown in economic growth.[34] Again, profitability plays a key role here. Even when demand is expanding fast, but the profit rate goes down, capital investment becomes sluggish. The semiconductor industry in the United States proves the point: Although there is a big (and growing) shortage of chips, capital investment is not following suit in rapid expansion of productive capacities, for during the last five years the industry has suffered a 31 percent fall in its average return on equity funds and an 18 percent decline in pretax profit margins.[35]

Likewise, the role and the strategy of the monopolies cannot be dissociated from this situation. The need to assure first a full depreciation of the gigantic capital investment realized in the previous wave (e.g., nuclear energy and nuclear power equipment) makes it extremely unlikely that capital outlays of the same amount can rapidly be introduced in competing sectors (e.g., solar energy).[36]

Third, further increases in the velocity of turnover of capital became more difficult. The revolution in telecommunications permitted the transfer of huge sums of money in only a few seconds from New York to Tokyo or from London to Johannesburg (which is still happening every day, all the cant about barbarous apartheid notwithstanding). But further progress in such areas as transportation, sales of goods, and turnover of liquid holdings has become increasingly scarce for more than a decade, partly for technical reasons but especially for socioeconomic reasons, because they run contrary to institutional social barriers linked to the very nature of capitalism: private property, bourgeois (i.e., highly unequal and class-biased) norms of distribution, and the survival of the nation-state.

Fourth, the long period of accelerated growth created conditions of increased disproportion between the rate of increase in productive capacity in fixed capital equipment and consumer goods, on the one hand, and that same rate of increase in the raw materials sector, on the other hand, which is still more closely tied to natural conditions and therefore less flexible. As a result, it became impossible to maintain for an indefinite period the decline in relative raw materials prices that had been occurring for nearly twenty years (1952–71). The real turning point here was the year 1972, not the rise in the price of oil after the Yom Kippur war. This reversal of the relationship of raw materials and energy prices to the prices of manufactured products is also related to the changed relationship of forces between the imperialist and the semicolonial bourgeoisie, a by-product of twenty-five years of upsurge in national liberation movements, without this change modifying the conditions of dependence of that bourgeoisie on imperialism. But all these factors undoubtedly had an adverse effect on the average rate of profit of industrial capital.

Strangely enough, W. W. Rostow saw in this very limited redistribution of surplus value on a world scale in favor of the ruling classes of the semicolonies the source for a new long-term upsurge in economic growth.[37] Leaving aside the fact that the magnitude of this redistribution is greatly exaggerated (the net gains of the OPEC countries must be set against the net losses of most of the non-oil-exporting semicolonial countries, which continue to be enormous), and the consideration that one should not confuse real redistribution of profits (oil rents) with increased credits for semicolonies (which translate themselves into increased debts, increased debt burdens, and therefore, in the medium term, into stagnation if not reduction in purchasing power on the world market, not at all an increase in such purchasing power), the main weakness of the argument is that it does not take into account the effect of the relative increase in raw materials prices on the rate of profit. This overall effect is negative. More expensive raw materials and energy costs mean a higher organic composition of capital and, all other things remaining equal, a lower average rate of profit. This cannot be offset by the higher rate of profit accruing to capital invested in the raw materials sector (e.g., the big oil monopolies), unless this capital should represent a high proportion (around 50 percent) of total invested capital, which is not at all the case.

The only positive effect of the long-term reversal of the terms of trade between raw materials and manufactured goods, in the framework of a capitalist economy, was that it stimulated the search for alternative materials and sources of energy (i.e., it favors innovation). But what scope that can

70

take and what impact that will have on the general trend in the rate of growth depend again on relative profitability. Only when investment in these fields promises to lead to important surplus profits (of such magnitude as to lead to a significant rise in the average rate of profit) can one expect this indirect effect of the rise in raw materials prices to favor an overall rise in the rate of growth of the international capitalist economy. But such superprofits in alternative technologies are not at all on the agenda, at least not for periods of short or medium duration and in sufficient amounts. On the contrary, alternative sources of energy are still much more expensive than expensive oil. So Rostow's analysis must be considered wrong. It obviously does not correspond to any visible trend in the international economy in the 1970s and 1980s, which have been characterized by declining, not rising, rates of growth.[38]

Fifth, during the whole expansionist long wave, potential overproduction (i.e., the development of productive capacity outgrowing the rise in purchasing power of the final consumers) was steadily building up. The best indicator of this is the steady decline of capacity utilization of American industry, at the peak of each cyclic boom as well as at the bottom of each cyclic recession (Table 3.1). But this general downward trend in capital utilization[39] has been a more general tendency throughout the imperialist countries, as is clearly shown in Table 3.2. These figures are all the more meaningful because 1978 was a year of economic recovery, whereas the 1964–73 average includes several recession periods.

Table 3.1. Use of Capacity

Boom		Recession	
Year	Percent	Year	Percent
1966	92	1967	78
1968	86.5	1971	75
1972	78.5	1975 (March)	65

Source: See Mandel, E. *The Second Slump.* London, 1978, p. 26.

Table 3.2. Use of capacity in manufacturing industries (in percentage)

	Annual average 1964–73	First half of 1978
United States	85.4	83.1
Japan	92.6	85.8
West Germany	86	80.8
France	84.8	83.7
Canada	88.1	85.4
Italy	78.5	72.4

Source: Data from *Perspectives Economiques de l'OCDE*, No. 24, December 1978, p. 12.

In specific branches of industry, this situation of chronic overcapacity is particularly pronounced. We shall point out two examples: In steel, the Common Market countries expected, before the outbreak of the crisis, to sell around 185 million tons in 1980. Real sales will probably be below 145 million tons. Built-up capacity was for 230 million tons of steel in 1980. Given the foreseen level of sales, big slashes in excess capacity are being planned. As for key chemicals, over-capacity is shown in Figure 6. The nuclear power plant equipment building industry is suffering from a similar over-capacity. The graph in Figure 7 indicates the general decline in capacity utilization in the United States in the decade 1965–75.

The steady growth in consumer debt during this same quarter century, as previously mentioned, is no less convincing an indicator of the same trend. This is especially obvious if we combine both factors: In spite of constantly increasing indebtedness, in spite of tens of millions of American consumers spending constantly more than they earn, a growing fraction of the productive capacity of the country is being laid idle. Massive unemployment also puts a brake on any rapid expansion of consumer expenditure of such a nature as to be able to overcome productive overcapacity.

Sixth, given all the previously mentioned growing contradictions, the only remaining means for capital to neutralize their effects on the average rate of profit (i.e., to avoid

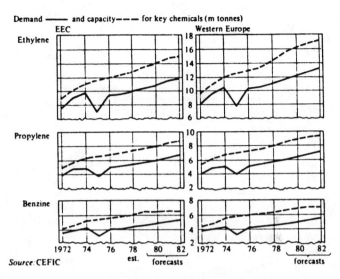

Figure 6. Overcapacity in key chemicals. Adapted from *The Economist*, April 7, 1979.

constant erosion of profitability) would have been a constant and heavy increase in the rate of surplus value. Although such an increase undoubtedly occurred in the first part of the expansionist long wave (in the same way as it had occurred before inception of the long wave, and thus had triggered off the long wave, so to speak) as a result of a steep rise in the productivity of labor in department II (increase in relative surplus value), with the cumulative effects of the expansionist long wave on the industrial reserve army of labor and on the degree of self-confidence and organization of the working class becoming operative since the early 1960s, it became increasingly difficult to keep up the momentum of the rise in the rate of surplus value. This rise began to run into the dual barriers of the end of the revolutionary phase of technological change and relative full employment. Precisely at the moment that the rise in the organic composition of capital quickened, the rise in the rate of surplus value slowed down. The fall in the rate of profit became unavoidable.

Seventh, under the conditions of increasing difficulties of

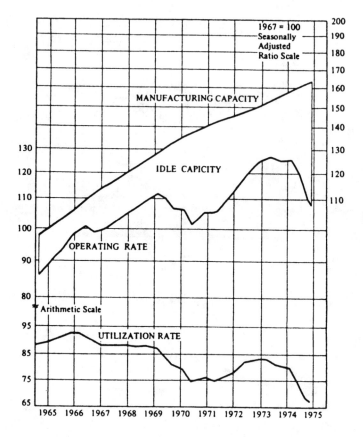

Figure 7. Declining capacity utilization in the United States (1967 = 100, seasonally adjusted ratio scale). Adapted from Systems Dynamics National Project, annual report 1976, p. 5.

realization combined with declining profitability, the function of inflation as a means to postpone the hour of reckoning could be kept operational only if the doses of inflation rose from cycle to cycle. But experience confirms what theoretical analysis predicted: Starting from a given level of inflation, its continuous acceleration becomes counterproductive for its effects on economic expansion. This is so for a great number of reasons, several of which deserve particular mention: the snowballing anticipatory reactions, the negative rate of "real" interest, the tendency to make long-term investment projects more dubious (and therefore more difficult) from the point of view of profit calculations and expectations.

Eighth, the continuous growth of the multinational corporation as the typical organization form of the late capitalist firm increasingly conflicts with the limited efficiency of economic intervention by the late capitalist state, countercyclic economic programming, and many other techniques through which the contradictions of the system had been partially reduced during the expansionist long wave. If we combine the seventh and eighth factors (growing, and nationally different, rates of inflation; growing weakness of the nation-state before the multinationals), we also integrate some of the more obvious technical reasons for the collapse of the Bretton Woods monetary system, as well as the resulting increasing international monetary anarchy, into our analysis.

Long Waves as Specific Historical Periods

Having outlined all these basic characteristics of the Marxist theory of the long waves of capitalist development, we have to draw a final conclusion. The long waves are not just empirically demonstrable. They do not simply represent statistical averages for given time spans. There is nothing "formal" or "conventional" (i.e., in the last analysis, arbitrary) about them, as there obviously is in the famous Kuznets long-term trends. They represent historical realities, segments of the overall history of the capitalist mode of production that have definitely distinguishable features. For that very same reason, they are of irregular duration.[1] The Marxist explanation of these long waves, with its peculiar interweaving of internal economic factors, exogenous "environmental" changes, and their mediation through sociopolitical developments (i.e., periodic changes in the overall balance of class forces and intercapitalist relationship of forces, the outcomes of momentous class struggles and of wars) gives this historical reality of the long wave an integrated "total" character.[2]

We can find an outstanding confirmation of this historical "totality" of the long waves in the correlation between a series of predominant ideologic trends (predominant within the framework of bourgeois ideology, at least) and the general trends of economic development that they reflect through a given prism.

Is it not remarkable how, throughout the whole period of accelerated economic growth of 1948–68, the credo of "growth optimism," "guaranteed full employment," and "technological rationality" reigned supreme, both within the realm of academic economics and sociology and among economic advisors and economic policy shapers? And when we passed from the expansionist long wave toward the depressive long wave, isn't it a striking coincidence that there suddenly appeared so many prophets of doom and of "zero growth"?

While we are willing to give great weight to the opinions of our learned colleagues engaged in counseling the various governments of the imperialist countries, we surely cannot exaggerate their role in bringing about decisive turning points in the economic development and in the trends of industrial output and world exports. We therefore conclude that it was the turn from the expansionist long wave to the depressive long wave that determined in the last analysis the turn from the Keynesian priority of full employment to the monetarist priority of fighting inflation. It was not the predominant economic doctrine that changed economic reality. It was the change in economic reality that changed the predominant economic doctrine.

But, again, in order to understand the total integrated character of the long waves, it is necessary to include the imperatives of the class struggle as major mediators between the basic trends of economic development and the basic trends of economic and sociopolitical ideology.

The general acceptance of Keynesian and neo-Keynesian ideas in the post-World War II period expressed both a certain assessment of the capitalist class in regard to the sociopolitical relationship of forces between capital and labor and a certain prediction on behalf of that same class as to the expansionist possibilities of the system. Within the framework of above-average long-term economic growth, full employment policies, although being moderately inflationary, would not upset the apple cart (i.e., would not basically threaten capitalist profits).[3]

The turnabout of academic economics toward the anti-Keynesian counterrevolution was not so much a belated recognition of the long-term threats of permanent inflation. These threats had been well known long before Keynesianism

77

lost its hegemony among economic advisors of bourgeois and reformist governments. It wasn't even essentially a product of the unavoidable acceleration of inflation, although undoubtedly this acceleration started to create panicky reactions in the early 1970s among theoreticians and practitioners of the capitalist economy alike. *It was essentially a product of a basic switch in class struggle priorities of the capitalist class.*

During an expansionist long wave, under conditions of rapid economic growth, and given a basic deterioration in the international relationship of forces at the expense of world capitalism, the priority for the capitalist class was to buy off the working class through reforms, among which full employment and social security policies played a key role. The economic expansion itself created the material conditions in which, by and large, the system could deliver these goods.

But when we pass from an expansionist long wave to a depressive long wave, it is no longer possible to assure full employment, to eradicate poverty, to extend social security, to assure a steady (if modest) increase in real income for the wage earners. At that point the fight to restore the rate of profit through a strong upswing in the rate of surplus value (i.e., the rate of exploitation of the working class) becomes the top priority.

The monetarists' "anti-Keynesian counterrevolution" in the realm of academic economics is nothing but the ideological expression of this changed priority. Without the long-term restoration of chronic structural unemployment, without the restoration of the "sense of individual responsibility" (i.e., without severe cutbacks in social security and social services), without generalized austerity policies (i.e., stagnation or decline in real wages), there can be no sharp rapid restoration of the rate of profit: That is the new economic wisdom.[4] There is nothing very "scientific" about it, but there is a lot that corresponds to the immediate and long-term needs of the capitalist class, all references to objective science notwithstanding.

Professor Heilbroner noted a rhythmic long-term alternation

between euphoria and despair among capitalists.[5] From our point of view, these are obviously consequences, not causes, of the switch from an expansionist long wave to a depressive long wave. But we can note a similar correspondence between the turn from one long wave to another, on the one hand, and the general ideological climate, by no means limited to economics, on the other hand.

In the interwar period, with its typical stagnating climate, and under the shock of World War I and the Russian revolution, there was a general switch to irrationality and mysticism among the intellectuals of many imperialist countries, especially in continental Europe and Japan (in the Anglo-Saxon countries, this trend was less pronounced, but by no means altogether absent). This was in sharp contrast to the atmosphere of optimistic faith in rationalism, the natural sciences, and human progress that prevailed during the pre-World War I period. In fact, in most European countries and in Japan, fascist or fascist-like doctrines conquered hegemony among university students and even university professors long before fascism conquered political power.

In the 1948–68 period there was a powerful reversal of that trend. In spite of the tremendous catastrophes that mankind had witnessed in the previous years (Hitler and Stalin, Auschwitz and Hiroshima), again there prevailed an atmosphere of optimism, faith in the natural sciences, belief in more or less unlimited economic growth, leading to more or less unlimited human progress. In that atmosphere, forces on the right wing and the extreme right wing were everywhere in retreat at the university level. And a combination of historical factors gave the student generation of the late 1960s an exceptional massive left-wing and pro-Marxist impetus, the like of which had never been encountered in the history of the bourgeois university.

With the turn from the expansionist long wave to the stagnating long wave, this has again changed. The "new philosophers" in France are but an example of a more general reversal toward the skepticism, irrationality, and mysticism that again prevail in many intellectual circles. This is by no means limited to the "lunatic fringe." On the contrary, a powerful offensive is under way to make social Darwinism, sociobiology, and the "scientific" justification of racism and of social inequality again respectable in academic circles. That offensive simultaneously penetrates deep into the inner circles of ruling political parties of the bourgeoisie, conservative and even "liberal-conservative" ones.[6] It is accompanied by a no less powerful upsurge in irrational, human-despising, and degrading trends in popular "subculture," of which astrology and "satanism" are but two striking examples,[7] again very similar to what happened in Germany and other countries in the early 1930s.

Certainly there is no mechanical parallel between the ups and downs of the student movement and the youth radicalization, on the one hand, and these significant shifts inside bourgeois ideology and ideological trends predominant inside the universities, on the other hand. The objective basis of youth radicalization and student radicalization continues to operate on a long-term basis, even if they are conjuncturally counteracted by massive youth unemployment, pressure to prepare for getting jobs at all costs, fear of not getting jobs, and disappointment with the delay in an overall political solution to the social crisis in which they are so deeply involved (i.e., disappointment with the historical delay of socialist revolution).

Likewise, there is no reason to identify the growing suspicion of the risks involved in capitalist technology and the capitalist misuse of the natural sciences with a general retreat into irrationalism, mysticism, despair, and disdain for the human race. We socialists and Marxists do not share the irresponsible "productivist" credo of the 1950s and 1960s. Many social criticisms of that credo are amply justified. One has not necessarily to accept the predictions of unavoidable absolute scarcity of energy and raw materials of the Club of Rome type[8] in order to understand that there is a collective responsibility for the present generation of humanity to transmit to future generations an environment and a stock of natural wealth that constitute the necessary precondition for the survival and flowering of human civilization. Neither has one to accept the impoverishing implications of permanent asceticism and austerity, so alien to the basic spirit of Marxism, which is one of enjoyment of life and infinite enrichment of human potentialities, in order to understand that the endlessly growing output of an endless variety of more and more useless commodities (increasingly, outright harmful commodities, harmful both to the environment and to the healthy development of the individual) does not correspond to a socialist ideal. Such an output simply expresses the needs and greeds of capital to realize bigger and bigger amounts of surplus value, embodied in an endlessly growing mountain of commodities.

But the rejection of the capitalist consumption pattern, combined with a no less resolute rejection of capitalist technology, should base itself from a socialist point of view on a vigorous struggle for alternative technologies that will extend, not restrict, the emancipatory potential of machinery (i.e., the possibility of freeing all human beings from the burden of mechanical, mutilating, non-creative labor, of facilitating rich development of the human personality for all individuals on the basis of satisfaction of all their basic material needs). We are convinced that once that satisfaction is assured in a society where the incentives for personal enrichment, greed, and competitive behavior are withering away, further "growth" will be centered around needs of "nonmaterial" production, (i.e., the development of richer social relations). Moral and psychological needs will supersede the tendency to acquire and accumulate more material goods. However "impopular" these beliefs may appear in the light of present-day fashions, we believe in the growing capacities of human intelligence, human science, human progress, human self-realization (including self-control), and human freedom, without in any way subordinating the defense of such freedoms (in the first place, freedom from want, but also freedom of thought, of creation, of political and social action) to any paternalistic instance supposedly capable of securing them for mankind.

But whatever may be these reservations, the correlation between a fundamental shift from the expansionist long wave toward the depressive long wave, and the no less fundamental shift in the prevailing mood among bourgeois ideologues, is too striking to be considered coincidental. The anti-humanist, anti-egalitarian and anti-democratic implications of this shift are ominous enough. They tie in with no less ominous long-term needs of international capital in the framework of a depressive long wave.

We can therefore accept the idea that the long waves are much more than just rhythmic ups and downs in the rate of growth of the capitalist economy. They are distinct historical periods in a real sense. The following tabulation clearly illustrates this:

1. 1789–1848: Period of the Industrial Revolution, of the great bourgeois revolutions, of the Napoleonic wars, and of the constitution of the world market for industrial goods: "upward" swing 1789–1815(25); "downward" swing 1826–48.
2. 1848–93: Period of "free-competition" industrial capitalism: "upward" swing 1848–73; "downward" swing 1873–93 (long depression of free-competition capitalism).
3. 1893–1913: Heyday of classic imperialism and finance capital; "upward" swing."[9]
4. 1914–40: Beginning of the epoch of decline of capitalism, of the epoch of imperialist wars, revolutions, and counterrevolutions; "downward" swing.
5. 1940(48)–?: Late capitalism born out of the historical delay of world revolution and the great defeats of the working class in the 1930s and 1940s, but accompanied by further phenomena of decline and decomposition of the system: "upward" swing (but limited to a significantly reduced geographic area) 1940(48)–67; "downward" swing 1968–?

The following question can be asked: Does the violent explosion of the inner contradictions of the capitalist mode of production after a lengthy period during which they have been repressed imply that the new long wave of relative stagnation or low growth is here to stay for an indefinite period and that a new turning point, similar to that of 1940(48) or 1893, is unlikely to appear in the foreseeable future, given the general historical framework of decline and decay of the international capitalist system? Or, in the opposite sense: In spite of the historical decline of the capitalist system, can it still repeat its "miracle" of 1940(48) and, after a long "cleansing" period throughout the 1970s, 1980s, and 1990s,[10] open up a new period of accelerated expansion comparable to that of the 1893–1913 period, if not that of the 1948–68 period?

These questions should be answered on two different levels. What are the "technical" requirements for such a new long wave of expansion? What is the social and political price that will have to be paid for it and, more generally, the price in terms of human welfare and human civilization?

From a technical point of view, a new expansionist wave that would significantly increase the rate of economic growth above the average levels of the 1970s, 1980s, and 1990s would require an explosive increase in the rate of accumulation and therefore in the average rate of profit and a no less remarkable expansion in the market for capitalist commodities in the most general sense of the word.

The "rationalization" function of the long wave of slower growth that we have been witnessing since the late 1960s and early 1970s would have to create the necessary economic preconditions for such a long-term sharp increase in the average rate of profit. Essentially, this would require the following: chronic mass unemployment tending in the long run to erode real wages and workers' self-confidence, militancy, and level of organization and to significantly increase the intensity of labor, leading toward a sharp upward shift in the rate of surplus value; massive devalorization of capital through increasing elimination of inefficient firms, not only small and

medium-size firms but also large ones, including many multinationals (i.e., through a new leap forward not only in national
but especially in international concentration and centralization of capital); new radical reductions, at least relatively, in the
costs of equipment, raw materials, and energy; massive applications of new technological innovations; a new revolutionary
acceleration in the rate of turnover of capital.

Theoretically, such radical changes in technology, work
organization, and circulation technique are possible; the
groundwork for them has already been laid by all the recent
developments in microprocessing. This would imply a new
qualitative leap forward in automation (i.e., a massive transition from semiautomation to automation). Likewise, genetic
engineering techniques could lead to radical innovations in
agriculture, pharmaceutics, scientific equipment, and a score
of other branches of industry.[11]

But two questions are immediately raised in this connection, from the point of view of value relations (i.e., from the
point of view of the overall laws of motion of the capitalist
mode of production and its internal logic).

In the first place, new radical substitution of machines for
men (in fact, the new wave of automation could be characterized as "robotism"[12]) would almost unavoidably imply
massive reduction in total productive employment. Estimates
on that subject vary greatly, but the overall trend is unmis-
takable. Overall studies of the effects of robotism in West
Germany have reported the reduction in wage earners made
possible by that technique at 4.3 workers per robot.[13]
Japanese studies have estimated that robotism could eliminate
one-third of presently existing industrial workers' jobs within
ten years and 90 percent of these jobs within twenty to thirty
years.[14]

Such a radical reduction in productive labor would most
probably imply a sharp drop in the *mass* of surplus value,
even if a new advance in the productivity of labor and a trend
toward stagnation or even decline in real wages should
strongly increase the production of relative surplus value (the

84

fraction of the total work week during which the workers produce the equivalent of the goods they buy with their wages). Under such conditions, an increase in the rate of surplus value could only be marginal, in no way proportional to the tremendous new outlays necessary for financing robotism. The rate of profit would not undergo a strong increase.

It seems unrealistic, to say the least, that the enormous mass of workers expelled from the production process by such revolutionary techniques could be reabsorbed through new expansion in the so-called service industries. On the contrary, one of the main effects of generalized application of microprocessing would be radical suppression of jobs in office work, administration, telecommunications, and even teaching. Experts in West German trade union circles have estimated that 75 percent of the 2.5 million employees engaged today in typing could be replaced by programmed mechanical letter production.[15] Whole professions like those of accountants, technical designers, and bank employees would be devastated if not completely suppressed. As the microprocessing equipment industry is itself likely to be revolutionized by massive introduction of automation, it could not provide the additional jobs needed to absorb the workers and employees expelled from other branches.

This is all the more so as one of the reasons for the slowdown in "average social productivity of labor" (a formula not very meaningful from a Marxist point of view) in countries like the United States, Great Britain, Sweden, etc. (i.e., the most industrialized ones) has been the strong increase in employment in the so-called service industries (especially government services, health services, and education). Hence the strong pressure to "rationalize" these services and make them "profitable" (the French term generally used, "rentabiliser," is particularly eloquent as to the inherent anti-humanist nature of capitalism: Make health and education services again "profitable!") through savage slashes in employment.[16]

So the overall balance sheet for a qualitative leap forward in automation (in fact, the transition from semiautomation to automation) through massive application of microprocessing would show a radical increase in permanent unemployment. Even if there should be an average annual growth rate of 3 percent in the coming ten years (which seems to discount new recessions and is far too optimistic), the conservative West German IFO institute for conjunctural studies has predicted 3.8 million unemployed in West Germany, if the previously sketched trends continue to expand. Sir Charles Carter, vice-chancellor of Lancaster University and chairman of the research and management committee of the Policy Studies Institute, London, is no less pessimistic:

> I believe unemployment will rise or remain high. . . . The new technology that was now being introduced was genuinely different in its impact compared with all previous technological changes. The service sector would not absorb those employed in manufacturing.[17]

American managers have expressed similar opinions. British trade unionists even speak about 5 million unemployed in their country by the end of the century, a figure *The Economist* finds wildly exaggerated, without denying that there is a problem and that "something will have to be done."[18]

Now, without even considering the explosive political and social consequences of such permanent unemployment, it is evident that it would create tremendous problems of realization of surplus value. The new technology would imply a new qualitative leap forward of the mass of use values produced (both old ones and new ones). Who is going to buy that huge mountain of goods, under conditions of massive unemployment inside the imperialist countries? Unfortunately for the capitalists, robots don't buy goods. And if that huge mountain includes a qualitatively higher amount of producers' goods (bought by surplus value), wouldn't such a radical reversion of the division of the national income again imply very violent social and political struggles? Wouldn't it, in any case, unavoidably lead to an increase in the mass of consumer goods produced after a certain time lag? The strong increase in productivity of labor that it would imply cannot but express itself in a massive increase in goods produced in the consumer goods sector too.

On the other hand, a new powerful expansion in the market for the commodities produced by the imperialist countries would require either a leap forward in industrialization (and welfare!) in some of the key semicolonial countries and areas in the world (the most heavily populated countries of Latin America, Asia, and Africa) or a qualitative increase in the degree of integration of the USSR and China into the international capitalist market, or a combination of both.

It is sufficient to enumerate these technical conditions to understand that they cannot be fulfilled by technical means alone. They will not come about as automatic products of certain economic changes, of current economic developments. Their realization, at least on a scale sufficient to unleash a new process of long-term accelerated growth in the international capitalist economy, would require momentous changes in the sociopolitical relationships of class forces within a whole series of key capitalist countries themselves, as well as on an international scale. In other words, whether or not they will be realized will depend on the outcome of social and political struggles that will mark the coming years, in the same way that at least some of these struggles have already marked recent years.

The worldwide offensive of capital against labor started under the sign of so-called austerity policies, and the return to chronic massive unemployment has undoubtedly the objective function of making possible sharp and long-term increases in the rate of surplus value and the rate of profit.[19] This offensive has had some success. For some years, real wages actually declined in a series of important industrialized capitalist countries, such as the United States, West Germany, Britain, and to some extent France and Italy. The intensification of the labor process is everywhere sharply increased, and with it the rate of exploitation of the working class, even where real wages continue to rise, but at a much slower rate than before.

87

However, the overall balance sheet of this capitalist success is very modest, to say the least. In France and Italy, the stubborn resistance of the unions and key sectors of the working class has resulted in only underprivileged and badly organized sections of the wage earners feeling the brunt of the employers' offensive, while the stronger ones have practically held their ground. The same probably is true, by and large, for North America, Germany, and Japan.

So one can say that in order to drive up the rate of profit to the extent necessary to change the whole economic climate, under the conditions of capitalism, the capitalists must first decisively break the organizational strength and militancy of the working class in the key industrialized countries. This would require a long period, as it did in the 1920s and 1930s. It would require in the United States breaking the backs of huge and powerful trade unions that did not even exist with the onset of the crisis of 1929. It would unavoidably imply social and political tests of strength involving huge class forces, millions if not tens of millions on the side of the wage earners at least.[20]

The important point to stress is that such a drive would imply radical curtailment of the democratic freedoms currently enjoyed in most of the imperialist countries. The numbers of representative spokespersons of the capitalist class who have confirmed this have become impressive. The previously quoted speech of Sir Charles Carter stated unequivocally that unemployment caused by new technology, coupled with continual inflation, could result in a breakdown of law and order and collapse of the present political system. W. W. Rostow claimed no less unequivocally that the solution lies in a middle way between the welfare economy and the warfare economy.[21] And most ominous of all are the trends spelled out in the report of the Trilateral Commission, *The Crisis of Democracy*, which reflect the convictions of a significant sector of the top leaders of international monopoly capital. They imply a direct attack on "excessive democracy," and they express the conviction that the types of decisions that will have to be taken in the coming years (in the interests of the capitalist system, obviously) and the very "governmentability" of the imperialist countries will depend on curtailment of democratic freedoms.[22]

Of course, one cannot beforehand exclude the possibility that decisive tests of strength between capital and labor will once again end with shattering defeats for the working class, as they did in the 1920s and 1930s. Nor can one exclude the possibility that new terrorist dictatorships, not necessarily identical to those of Mussolini, Hitler, Franco, or the Japanese military caste of the 1930s and early 1940s, but similar to them in their effects of destroying working-class organization and democratic freedoms, might be used by the ruling class to reach the desired effect of strongly reducing the relative weight of wages in the national income. But one should point out that the relationship of forces between capital and labor is much more favorable today to labor than it was in the 1923–40 period, both internationally and in all countries concerned nationally if one takes only the objective criteria into consideration, and in most countries (with the possible exceptions of West Germany and the United States) if one adds to them the subjective factor.

In any case, inflicting such shattering defeat on the working class is impossible in the short run. This could only come about as the end result of some period of skirmishes and preliminary struggles through which labor's strength would be eroded, while at the same time no significant progress would be realized in the field of raising the average level of class consciousness and the capacity of the working class to produce a growing vanguard of radicalized workers who would contribute decisively to the appearance of a new leadership and new revolutionary parties capable of rising to the level of responsibility demanded by the very nature of the tests of strength to be faced. Personally, we believe that there is not the slightest ground for pessimistic conclusions of that sort on the basis of what has occurred in most of the key imperialist countries during the last ten years, including West Germany and the United States (where the emergence of that layer has been slower than in other countries, but by no means absent).

Similar remarks are pertinent if we look at the question of geographic expansion of markets. Radical rather than marginal changes in the transformation of some key areas in the so-called third world into large markets for capitalist commodities would require radical changes in the internal social structures of these countries,[23] radical defeats of national liberation movements, and huge successes in a first phase of industrialization of such extent that a change from a repressive to a reformist policy (from a decrease to an increase in the standard of living of 75% of the population) would become materially possible for the ruling class. The least one can say is that there are very few indications that such momentous changes are about to occur, even in countries like Brazil or Mexico, not to mention India, Pakistan, Indonesia, Nigeria, and Egypt. In smaller countries like Venezuela, Kuwait, Hong Kong, Singapore, and Taiwan, this is, of course, possible and is already occurring; but its effects on the world market as a whole remain absolutely marginal.[24]

One should not confuse an overall expansion in the world market at a rapid phase with an overall restructuring of the international capitalist division of labor. If a big shift of the textile industry, the petrochemical industry, or the industry of assembling light electronic equipment occurs from imperialist countries toward semi-industrialized countries, this in no way implies automatic expansion in the world market. Employment at lower wages in certain countries is substituted for employment at higher wages in other countries. Equipment is shifted from one part of the world to another. The overall effect on aggregate demand will remain indifferent. In the best of cases, it will mean a marginal increase in aggregate demand as a result of a higher multiplier operating in semi-industrialized countries as against the metropolis, starting from an identical initial investment. But all this is absolutely insufficient to unleash, by itself, a new long-term wave of accelerated growth, especially if one takes into consideration the fact that most of the branches of industry shifting toward semi-industrialized countries are already faced with near-saturation of worldwide demand.[25]

It is even possible that such a restructuring of the international capitalist division of labor has an overall positive effect on employment in the imperialist countries, the increase in jobs in their equipment exporting industries more than neutralizing the loss of jobs in the industries shifting to the third-world countries, as a recent OECD study contended.[26] But this effect is so modest and so out of proportion to the magnitude of the total level of present unemployment (not to mention the unemployment foreseen if microprocessing becomes generalized) that it can in no way provide the basis for a rapid or medium-term transcending of the depressive long wave.

If one considers the possibility of huge expansions of markets in the postcapitalist countries, one must take into consideration that despite the huge success of the German *Ostgeschäft* (to which one can now add, with the necessary caution, the similar success of Japan's China business), the total part of the "socialist" countries in exports of imperialist countries was less than 5 percent in 1977.[27] For this to expand to perhaps 10 to 12 percent and significantly increase the annual rate of growth of the capitalist world market, there would have to occur a huge credit explosion, which would involve several hundreds of billions of dollars, more than the West's credit explosion to the so-called third-world countries in the second half of the 1970s. Without even examining the effects of such a credit explosion on the average international rate of inflation and the permanent crisis in the reserve paper currencies, one should point out that such a huge structural change in these countries' relations with the international capitalist economy would also mean a radical weakening of their capacity for long-term economic planning independent of the fluctuations in the international capitalist economy and a radical change in the internal power structure, which would probably require important social and political upheavals, if not outright wars by imperialism (not necessarily nuclear wars).

Here, again, we do not want to minimize the changes that have already occurred, the significant growth in East-West trade and in capitalist cooperation investment projects in the so-called socialist countries, of which the growing involvement of the Teng regime in China with the capitalist West (above all, Japan) is going to mean a new significant extension. But what we contend is that without radical upheavals of the type just indicated, their overall effects on the international capitalist economy will remain limited, not of sufficient amplitude to unleash the dynamic of a long wave of accelerated growth in that economy.

Thus our general conclusion is that the "technical" possibility of a new strong upturn in the long-term rate of capitalist growth will depend on the outcomes of momentous battles between capital and labor in the West, between capital and labor in some of the key semi-industrialized countries of the so-called third world, between the national liberation movements and imperialism, and between the noncapitalist countries and imperialism (on which the internal struggles between the masses and the bureaucratic rulers of these countries will also have effects), if not a series of international wars and civil wars. Again, the similarity to the situation of the 1930s is striking. Again one should stress that the working class and the oppressed peoples of the world enter this period of violent upheavals under much more favorable conditions than they did in the late 1920s and 1930s, although by no means under ideal conditions.

It has often been said that Marxists, especially revolutionary Marxists, have greatly underestimated capitalism's capacity for flexible adaptation to new and radical challenges, such as changed social and international environments. Without wanting to deny that there is an element of truth in that criticism, at least when it is directed against certain dogmatic schools of thought referring to Marxism, we believe that the Marxist theory of the long waves of capitalist development integrates precisely this capacity into the overall history of the system. But it does more than that. It also points to the social and human costs of that adaptation, a factor that the apologists of the system generally cover up by discreet silence.

A huge outcry has been made about the human and social costs of the first "socialist" experiments, beginning with that of the Soviet Union, independent of whether or not one accepts the balance sheet of historical progress to which these experiments have led. We cannot, in the framework of this text, submit this method of historical book-keeping to the thorough criticism it certainly merits. Nor do we have the space here to prove that Stalin was by no means a necessary product of the October revolution and that if the huge massacres and waste caused by Stalin were not necessary to thoroughly industrialize and modernize Russia, the October revolution most certainly was. But let no one forget that the "adaptations" through which world capitalism went in order to overcome the crisis of stagnation of the 1920s and 1930s involved fascism, Auschwitz, and World War II and its huge destruction, punctuated by Hiroshima (i.e., at least 60 million dead, without taking into account the subsequent colonial wars and the millions of dead they caused, as well as the persistent misery and hunger in the "third world").[28] That is the social and human price mankind paid for capitalism's method of overcoming the Great Depression and embarking on a new phase of long-term expansion. Indeed, the formula "destructive adaptation" necessary for "creative destruction" is valid in this context![29]

When we said that one cannot exclude the theoretical possibility of a new phase of expansion starting with the 1990s, although it seems quite unlikely to us, one must add immediately that the social and human price of that "adaptation" would be, this time, incommensurably more costly than it was in the 1930s and early 1940s. This is true not only because the enemies of capitalism have become much stronger nationally and internationally than they were before (thus requiring much more violence and destruction to break their resistance) but also because the very nature of the technological environment (including nuclear weapons, but by no means only nuclear weapons or indeed only weapons) and the frightful dynamics of misery, hunger, and diseases have become potentially much more destructive than they were fifty or forty years ago.

One has only to compare the Pinochet dictatorship with the Alessandri one in Chile. One has only to imagine what it would mean to have a new Hitler capable of deploying nuclear weapons, to think about the possibility of totalitarian regimes using large-scale lobotomy or other contemporary neurosurgical methods to break their political opponents, to consider the possibilities of using international food reserves not only for purposes of blackmailing third-world countries but also for explicit purposes of limiting the rate of increase in the "third-world" population to get a feeling for the potential barbarism involved in a next stage of destructive "adaptation" of capitalism to its structural crisis, as a precondition for a new expansion.

And the objective function of the current resurgence in irrational and anti-humanist "values" in bourgeois culture and subculture is precisely to prepare people's minds for acceptance or at least passive "tolerance" of a possible next wave of barbarism. It both prepares it ideologically and anticipates it "ideally."[30]

We leave aside the question whether or not mankind's environment can support another fifty, not to say one hundred, years of economic growth of the type we have known during the 1940(48)–68 period, with its huge waste of natural resources and the growing threat to ecological equilibrium that it implies. We do not belong to the school of the prophets of doom. We believe that science and conscious human endeavor can solve any problem that science, subjugated to the private profit motive, has created. But it is clear that in a capitalist economy such solutions will not be applied, at least not on sufficient scale to prevent a new phase of accelerated anarchistic economic growth that would increase the many threats to our common future.

If one adds together all these threats and costs of the "destructive adaptation" (the only one that capitalism could achieve, under certain very improbable circumstances, and given a favorable outcome for the bourgeois class in all the momentous struggles that are already marking and will increasingly mark the long wave with a stagnating trend), one should conclude that instead of speculating about the possibility of such an "adaptation," it would be wiser to consider ways and means of avoiding it. A new "wave of economic growth" involving a few hundreds of millions of dead isn't exactly an ideal future to look forward to.

We are deeply convinced that there is another way out of this period of economic depression, a way that would reduce the social and human costs to a minimal fraction of capitalism's "destructive adaptation." This is the socialist way: appropriation by the producers of their means of production; their planned use for the purpose of directly satisfying needs, not making profits; determination of planning priorities by majority rule and democratic processes involving all democratic freedoms of information, choice, debate, contestation, and political pluralism; management of the economy by the associated producers themselves and of society by its citizens, organized in democratic bodies of self-administration; accelerated withering away of the bloated and costly bureaucratic state apparatus; rapid reduction of inequalities of income, and of money and market economy; radical reduction of the workday, without which self-management and self-administration are either utopian or humbug. This is what socialism, as conceived by Karl Marx (a regime of associated producers), is all about. It can only be realized on a broad international scale. It is the creative adaptation of mankind to the needs and possibilities of the present epoch, based on the conscious choice to avoid the costs of capitalism's spontaneous "destructive adaptation." We do not know if it will come about in time to avoid the disasters that face mankind in the next decades, but it is in any case the only way open to us to possibly avoid these disasters. To fight for it is the only rational, decent, generous course open to anyone who has not abandoned faith in the future of mankind and who desires to guarantee that future.

Old Problems and New Data:
an inventory of the international debate

Over the last hundred years there appears to have been a long wave of awareness of long waves which has run more or less "countercyclically" to the phenomenon itself. When the concept was launched by the Marxist economists Parvus and van Gelderen during the long expansion of 1893–1913, it hardly had any resonance among academic economists. Then, during the long interwar depression, the problematic came into its own with the pioneering work of Kondratieff and Schumpeter and the important contribution by Dupriez, as well as Trotsky's distinctive intervention in the debate.

Throughout the long boom that followed World War II, the theory of long waves was largely forgotten or dismissed as irrelevant. This author was almost the only exception when he predicted in the mid-1960s that the long expansion would lead to a new long depression, and that this would appear by the end of the 1960s or the early 1970s. With the onset of that depression, however, there has been an explosion of interest and debate around the issue of long waves. The number of books and articles in learned journals is so large that it is impossible to deal with each and every one of them.

This new mass of argument and data makes it necessary to clarify one point without delay. What are we really discussing? Long waves of what exactly? This is not a semantic question. For it is our view that long waves involve output, employment, and national income on an international scale; hence, basic trends of world trade. After all, the long wave concept was a by-product of business cycle theories, which deal with essentially the same matters. The explanation of long waves, then, cannot be divorced from the problem of recurrent crises of overproduction, themselves organically linked to the basic laws of motion of the capitalist mode of production.

As we argued in Chapter 1, the only "open" question in this respect is whether we should situate the first long wave in the 1820s, with the birth of what Marx himself called the world market for industrial goods, or whether the long depression that began at that time had been preceded by a long expansion roughly coinciding with the period of war between Britain and France in the wake of the French Revolution.

Kondratieff's theory started from long cycles of price fluctuation, and Andre Gunder Frank and especially Immanuel Wallerstein have pushed their analyses of such cycles back many centuries. If based upon empirical evidence, there is nothing illegitimate in this endeavor. It is then just a long wave theory of prices, nothing more.[1] But Wallerstein goes much further. On the basis of these price fluctuations, he constructs a unified long cycle theory of the world economy, which projects the uneven "core versus periphery" relationship, and not current surplus value production, as the main motor of capital accumulation on a world scale from at least the fifteenth century until the present day.[2] It thus assumes away the fundamental characteristic, if not the very existence, of the capitalist mode of production as such, based upon unpaid labor extracted from wage-laborers.

It is true that primitive accumulation of capital largely originated in plunder of the "periphery" by commercial capital of the "center." In that specific form of accumulation, there was direct or indirect transfer of a surplus product produced by other than wage labor, essentially the labor of peasants and independent handicraftsmen. After a certain point in history, however, the principal mass of surplus product fuelling capital accumulation, both on a world scale and in all key countries, became surplus value produced by wage labor. There is no empirical evidence that would lead us to reject

98

that definition. So our conclusion stands: the long waves at issue are long waves of capitalist development, coinciding in time with the hegemony of the capitalist mode of production and recognizable since the onset of the Industrial Revolution.

Another matter is the chronological framework that needs to be adopted. If the choice is arbitrary, it will be extremely difficult to find any statistical corroboration of "long waves" that does not beg the question. But from our own point of view "long waves" are not, for example, "averages" of first more and then less growth for random fifty-year periods, such as 1800–50, 1850–1900, 1900–50 and 1950–2000. They correspond to real historical periods. And whereas a chronology that abstracts from this reality can even make the great slump of 1929–40 disappear, the fact is that that slump was very real indeed.

Related to this is the problem of the so-called Kuznets swings, which Solomos Solomou has reintroduced into the current debate in an attempt to refute the theory of long waves. Kuznets's idea was of 20-to-25-year swings, episodic in character, longer than the normal business cycle but shorter than the postulated long waves.[3] Once again, however, this simply begs the question, substituting statistical series for causal analysis.

When Solomou says that I myself was "misled" by assuming a decline in the rate of profit as an explanation for the end of the postwar boom, he forgets that it was this which allowed me as early as 1964 to predict that the boom would come to an end in the late 1960s or early 1970s. How would this have been possible if the diagnosis had been so wide of the mark?

In opposition to my use of evidence for long waves drawn from Kuczynski, Solomou states: "Only if history is truncated at 1872 would it be possible to talk of a Kondratieff wave-phasing of world economic development."[4] But that is not what the data show. The "truncating" in 1872 corresponds to the beginning of a long depression,[5] which most historians consider to be an undeniable fact. It was followed by a period of expansion, with an average growth rate 50 percent higher than in the previous decades.

And would Solomou deny that the growth rate then sharply declined between the two wars, shot up again during the post-war boom, and has been radically lower again since the early 1970s? Are these not periods of irregular duration (1873–93, 1893–1913, 1914–40, 1940(48)–73, 1973–2000?), in no way reducible to a 22-year pattern? Above all, do they not correspond to an inner logic which, far from being purely episodic, has stood up rather well in the light of what has happened since our analysis was presented in the first edition of this book in 1980?

Solomou tries to explain the basically irregular patterns of economic growth over the past century and a half in terms of a "technology gap" which has led to "extremely irregular G-waves (shocked Gerschenkronian catching-up waves)," but which essentially results from technological gaps between the national economies. Other factors, such as credit inflation, he dismisses as largely irrelevant. And yet, events since the Mexican debt crisis and the 1987 stock exchange crash have laid that assumption to rest.

The weakness of Solomou's argument is most clearly revealed in its conclusion: "It should be emphasized that since a degree of relative backwardness still exists in the world economy, this is a sufficient condition for the G-wave growth path continuing into the future, once rapid economic growth is resumed."[6] Under what conditions? Solomou cannot answer such questions. But we did so in 1978 and are able to be even clearer today.

The exact periodization of the long waves is likewise a matter of controversy. Kleinknecht lists the attempts made in this respect by twelve different authors, and if he singles out my own it is because he regards it as the most orthodox and the one that includes world market trends.[7] He wants first of all to test the reality of long waves on the basis of statistical evidence. And roughly speaking, his conclusion is that there is convincing evidence of long waves for the world economy of the last hundred years, but not for the period before 1890. Kleinknecht's own evidence of detrended nine-year moving averages, however, clearly testifies to the reality of long waves. We give just one of his graphs: we could reproduce more.

Such trends are clearest for world output and for the output of the major industrial countries, the exception being the United States in the pre-1880 period, for well-known structural reasons. The only possible dispute is whether the extent of the fluctuations is such as to allow a long wave pattern to be identified. But for structural unemployment to increase dramatically, with all the consequences as to overproduction and excess capacity, it is sufficient that during a long depression the average rate of growth of output consistently falls below the average in the long expansion, while labor productivity continues to expand as before. A long wave pattern can, therefore, be recognized.

Here an important aspect of the long waves hypothesis must be taken into consideration: namely, the cumulative

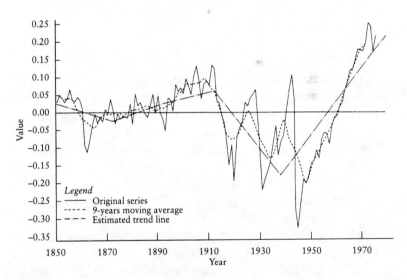

Figure 8. World industrial production: Including mining (Detrended with −41.62127 + 0.02519 year). Adapted from Kleinknecht (see Note 7, p. 156 this volume), p. 39.

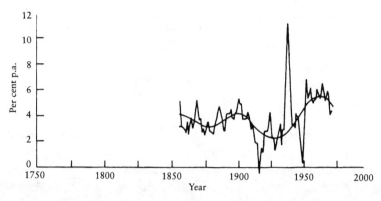

Figure 9. Capitalist world industrial production.[a] Adapted from Kuczynski, as quoted by Cleary and Hobbs, in Christopher Freeman, ed., *Long Waves in the World Economy.*

[a] Growth rate in percent p.a., 11-year moving average

nature of changes in the rate of growth. If the difference in annual growth rates between a long expansion and a long depression is only 1 percent or even less, the cumulative effect after twenty or twenty-five years is still undeniable.

Extensive evidence of long waves is offered in the book edited by Christopher Freeman,[8] as well as in Andrew Tylecote's book on the subject. Tylecote's periodization largely dovetails with our own, as do his historical comments and reservations regarding the United States. His remarks on Britain (where we made a mistake in Chapter 1, on which Van Duijn concentrated his criticism of the book as a whole) are likewise well taken. At the same time, however, Tylecote seems compelled by a general aversion to Marxism to accuse us of arguing that in the late 1940s there was "a radical change in the socio-political environment in which the system operates (destruction of trade unions, elimination of bourgeois democracy, atomization of the working class, impossibility of collective sale of the commodity labor power, etc.)."[9] This is a peculiar misreading of what we actually wrote. We never suggested that grave defeats of the working class occurred in the late 1940s. We situated them, rather, in the 1920s and 1930s (until 1942–43), involving in different degrees all the major imperialist countries except the United States, and most underdeveloped ones as well (principally China, India, and Latin America). During those two decades the rate of surplus value was greatly increased, and the resulting decline in the real consumption of the working class was *maintained until* (not brought about in) the late 1940s. Thus the long postwar boom began with both a high rate of profit and an expanding market, given that the real consumption of wage-earners could move sharply up from a low base.

A number of studies have attempted a more precise delineation of long waves in various national economies. The most striking of these is the work of Jesús Albarracín on the Spanish economy, but similar research has been done for France, Belgium, the United States, Canada, West Germany, Argentina, and Italy.[10] In the USSR, Eastern Europe, and the "official" Communist parties, economists long denied the

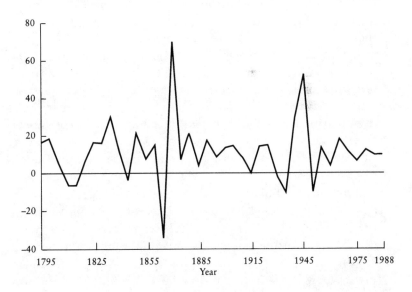

Figure 10. Peter Grimes of Johns Hopkins University has sent me this table that he drew up to represent the percentage growth of per capita GDP in the United States.

103

existence of long waves. But there too a change occurred in the 1970s, initiated by Jürgen Kuczynski in the GDR and Paul Boccara in the French Communist Party,[11] then picked up in the USSR by Stanislav Menshikov.[12] The situation in China is not clear, but this book has been published by one of the Beijing universities. The long night of Stalinist repression and straightforward thought-control made any serious scientific debate impossible in that milieu. With de-Stalinization, however, the long wave debate got under way again and picked up the controversies of the 1920s associated with the work of Kondratieff. One Soviet author has recently given an exhaustive summary of those disputes, which mostly turned on the issue of an automatic long-term upswing (i.e., the hypothesis of a long *cycle*) that Trotsky, for example, rejected from the outset. They carry no weight in relation to the theory of long *waves*.

As already stated, Richard Day accuses us of trying to make an eclectic and therefore inconsistent combination of Kondratieff and Trotsky. In fact, we specifically state that there is no symmetry between the turn from long expansion into long depression (which is essentially endogenous), and the turn from long depression into long expansion (which is not endogenous and requires "system shocks" from outside). Our own theory is distinctive then; it has to be judged on its own merits, verified or falsified in the light of historical evidence and its theoretical consistency. One can accept it. One can reject it. But one cannot treat it as an eclectic combination of other theories.

Day's mistake here is to link the long wave controversy to a policy issue that was part of the general economic debate in the CPSU and the USSR in the 1920s and early 1930s: that is, the question of the possibility and limitations of autarky in relation to the international capitalist economy. In that debate Trotsky and the Left Opposition (later the United Opposition) consistently argued against the possibility and usefulness of conceiving Russia's economic development independently of the world economy. Indeed, the impossibility of total insulation was one of the key arguments against the theory of completing the construction of socialism in one country. On this too we do not take an "eclectic" position: we are fully in agreement with Trotsky and always have been. But the important point here is that it in no way contradicts the theory of long waves of capitalist development. What it does imply is that the world market will have a different impact on Soviet economic development during long depressions and during long expansions of international capitalism. History has certainly confirmed that hypothesis.

When we use the concepts "endogenous" and "exogenous" in this context, we have to make clear exactly what we mean. Thus, if "exogenous" is defined in relation to bourgeois society, or to the capitalist mode of production in the broadest and most abstract sense, then of course there can be no grounds for dispute. The real problem (and the theoretical difficulty from a Marxist point of view) is whether the three long upswings beginning in 1849, 1893 and 1940(49) were inevitable products of the depressions that preceded them; or whether they occurred only as a result of "system shocks" such as wars, bourgeois revolutions, victorious counter-revolutions or sharp rises in gold production. Our own position is in favor of the second hypothesis, which seems to conform to the historical evidence.

As to Boccara and Menshikov, their valuable contributions to the theory of long waves both suffer from too rigid extrapolation from business cycle theory. Boccara's key concept is that of an alternation between overaccumulation and devalorization of capital. In the normal business cycle, this alternation is based upon the longevity of fixed capital and the growing physical and moral obsolescence endogenously induced toward the end of the boom. But as no major elements of fixed capital last for twenty to thirty years (with the exception of buildings and railways, which have certainly played no major role in investment for a century and more) it is not clear why their obsolescence would trigger increased long-term devalorization of capital, and thus a long depression.

Menshikov has constructed an ingenious model essentially based upon three variables: namely, the rates of growth of labor productivity, of capital intensity (capital stock per hour of labor actually expended), and of the rate of profit. Each of these variables, he argues, adjusts at a different rate. In essence, labor productivity adapts to capital intensity, and capital intensity to the rate of profit. This accounts for the endogenous, practically automatic, nature of the long-term movement. Oscillations are produced by the slow rhythms of adjustment. If the rate of profit is high, there is less need for labor-saving innovations; hence, a long expansion occurs. If the rate of profit is declining, new investment will also decline and a long depression will set in. Conversely, toward the end of the depression, innovations will increase and with them the rate of profit, so that in the end new investment outlays are driven up and a new long expansion is triggered off.

The basic assumption here is of a stable or near-stable rate of surplus value, so that the rate of profit is exclusively or essentially a function of fluctuations in the organic composition of capital. There is no empirical evidence for this, however. Quite the contrary: such equations simply eliminate the class struggle and its cumulative long-term effects, what Marx called the relative strength of the contenders. And when Menshikov accuses us of holding that capitalism overcame the long interwar depression through "accidents or tricks," "reforms or militarization," his formula borders on the absurd.[13] How can one consider Hitler's coming to power, Franco's victory in the Spanish Civil War, the massive arms drive in the United States, World War II, the postwar hegemony of US imperialism in the capitalist economy, or the Marshall Plan as "accidents or tricks"? What Menshikov presupposes is that a long depression which forces capitalism to renew its technology and forms of organization, including the organization of labor, will automatically succeed in imposing the burden of a new organization of labor (and many other things) upon the working class. This we deny.

Working like Forrester at the M.I.T. Systems Analysis

Center, John Sterman has constructed a simulation model in which long-term movements basically result from the impact on the economy as a whole made by investment decisions in the producer goods sector (Department I in Marx's reproduction tables).[14] The different long-term results then correlate with different rates of growth of sales to final consumers, that is, of Department II. At a certain degree of correlation between the two growth rates, excess capacity in Department I will develop fairly slowly in the course of several successive business cycles. If the disproportions become larger, then a cumulative growth of excess capacity will occur.

Sterman can base himself on empirical data from the history of the US economy to support his theory. But he does not sufficiently build into it the mediation of *ex ante* and *ex post* rates of profit. Less overcapacity and less physical obsolescence do not automatically lead to a growth of investment decisions, unless these are justified by "reasonable" expectations of profit. It is true that a growth in excess capacity and obsolescence in value terms automatically trigger lower rates of investment. But that only gives us an asymmetrical long-term movement: an endogenous turn from long expansion to long depression; and a turn from long depression to long expansion which is triggered by exogenous factors (system shocks) leading toward a sharp upturn in the anticipated and achieved rates of profit.

Anwar Shaikh's contribution to Marxist economic theory in general and to a Marxist explanation of long waves has been quite outstanding. Unfortunately, he goes astray on one important question. He writes:

> My argument is similar to Mandel's [in which long waves of accelerated and decelerated accumulation are direct expressions of corresponding long waves in the rise and decline of the rate of profit], with one crucial difference. Mandel's is a long wave theory based on up-and-down movements in the rate of profit. In contrast to this, I have long argued that Marx's theory of a secularly falling rate of profit provides a natural foundation for a theory of long waves.[15]

We have, of course, never denied the secular tendency of the average rate of profit to decline. But the history of capitalism does confront Marxists with a real challenge. In three periods, after 1848, after 1892, and after 1940(48), there has been an impressive long-term acceleration of capital accumulation, which from a Marxist point of view implies a no less impressive surge of the rate of profit. It is impossible to argue that this "expresses" in any way whatever the secular trend of the average rate of profit to decline. On the contrary, it temporarily breaks that trend.

Anwar Shaikh argues that what is relevant for the transition between long waves is the rising *mass* of profit. According to Marx, this rise does indeed partially dampen the effects of the declining average rate of profit upon capitalist business activity. However, Marx clearly states that it is only one among several such trends. It was and is our contention that at the very least all of these "countervailing forces" have to operate (besides the system shocks) for a long expansion to occur.

Anwar Shaikh's data themselves prove that this upturn in the rate of profit occurred during the postwar boom in US manufacturing. He then adds:

> Over the postwar period, the normal rate of profit displays a clear downward trend. But this is masked [!] by a 17-year wave in capacity utilization, which rises sharply from 1958–1966, and then declines just as sharply from 1966–1975. The actual rate of profit thus rises in the upturn of the postwar long wave, then falls in the downturn phase. Mandel would interpret this as evidence of a rise-and-fall in the actual rate of profit causing the long upturn and downturn. I would interpret it as an effect of a secularly falling rate of profit, in which this falling profitability eventually chokes off the long upturn.[16]

We have no dispute with the final part of the sentence. But it is beside the point. For the real problem is not what choked off the long expansion. The problem is what made it possible. Anwar Shaikh's graph 7.6 shows a sharp rise in the rate of

108

profit. What then caused the postwar boom? Simply an increase in capacity utilization? Why did that occur? Was it not also a function of expanding markets? And does this not bring us back to the operation of *all* "countervailing forces" in the totality mentioned above?

Rabah Benakouche asserts that our assumption of a rising organic composition of capital is not borne out by the empirical data, and in support of his argument he maintains that the organic composition of capital is reflected in the capital/output ratio.[17] This is incorrect. Gérard Duménil and Dominique Lévy have recently produced data for the United States which confirm a constant increase in the capital/labor ratio between 1869 and 1989: that is, for 120 years, even if the rhythm was much stronger in the 1869–1912 and 1951–89 periods and much weaker between 1912 and 1951.[18] The capital/labor ratio does not completely conform to the organic composition of capital, but it is closely related to it. And so we stand vindicated.

Benakouche makes the interesting point that the ups and downs of the rate of profit must be related to what he calls the organization of the labor process. We would prefer to stick to the classical Marxist terminology of the rate of surplus value. But at any event when he speaks of the relative "porosity of labor," he should have spelled out the central question. The possibility for capital to extract more surplus labor from productive wage labor depends upon the end-result of two contradictory movements: the rate of growth of labor productivity, which is the source of relative surplus value, and the capacity of the workers, through the ongoing class struggle, to increase the value (price of production) of labor power by incorporating into wages the purchasing power for additional goods and services. We shall return to this in the next chapter.

In point of fact, in the present slump the constantly rising mass unemployment results to a large degree from the constant rise in the productivity of labor under conditions of sharply reduced average rates of growth of output and income.

For the first edition of this book, we encountered difficulties in establishing statistical data on long-term fluctuations of profit rates properly so called. We therefore used interest rate fluctuations as an indicator (or reflection) of profit rates. But since then the studies of Duménil and Lévy have directly confirmed the long-term fluctuation in the profit rate in the United States.

One of the explanations for a persistent above-average profit rate during an expansionary long wave is the long-term availability of various sources of surplus profits, of which the most striking are technological rents and monopolistic rents. The fact that these are available is connected with the dialectic of scientific discoveries, technological innovation and technological diffusion, already dealt with in Chapter 2 of this book. We saw there that for Schumpeter, and later Gerhard Mensch as well as Van Duijn, Dosi and others, a "bunching" of technological innovations occurs toward the end of long depressive waves and is the main cause of an

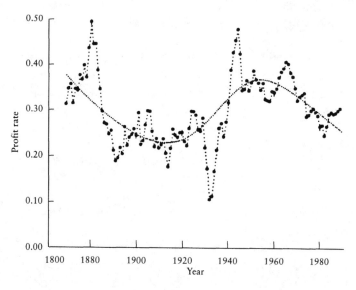

Figure 11. The historical profile of the profit rate and its trend (1869–1989). Adapted from Duménil and Lévy. [19]

110

expansionary long wave. To verify the Mensch/Van Duijn hypothesis, Kleinknecht has made a thorough examination of the existing data and of the present state of the controversy, basing himself especially on Mahdavi's evaluation of 120 major innovations.[20] After taking into consideration a number of criticisms, especially that of Clark, Freeman, and Soete,[21] Kleinknecht concludes that the "cluster of innovations" hypothesis is not called into question. He adds that a long depression is likely to have a contradictory influence upon the emergence of new technologies, on the one hand providing a strong incentive to strike out in new directions, but on the other hand increasing the risks involved in such a move. In Kleinknecht's view, the empirical evidence indicates that the "depression-trigger" mechanism is stronger than the inhibiting factors.[22] It is doubtful whether the conclusion is valid, however, at least in such a simplified form.

In order to rescue his initial position, which really involves a technological explanation of long waves, Mensch has advanced a more sophisticated account of the turn from long depression to long expansion.[23] He now considers that a key contributing factor is the incidence of disappointing depreciation of installed capital goods in stagnating industries. This induces investors to seek out alternatives, taking into account fluctuations in capacity utilization, and thus makes the system ready for new technologies.[24]

There is a gap in Mensch's argument, however. For massive (as distinct from exploratory) innovations to occur, there must be simultaneously a sharp rise in the rate of profit and a significant enlargement of the market. No massive investment outlays in new technologies and new products will occur as long as prospective sales remain below a certain threshold. We are talking of billions of units, if not more, sold throughout the world over several decades. So the question is not: Are new inventions available? or Have new innovations started? The question is: Are they of sufficient scope and sufficient duration to make possible a repetition of the postwar boom? The evidence so far clearly points in the opposite direction.

111

Neither billions of "ecologically clean" motor cars, nor billions of household or laser application robots are likely to be sold in the foreseeable future. To be sure, the electric car has gone beyond the purely experimental stage.[25] So have new advances in biotechnology. But their massive introduction (and thus the massive appearance of technological rents) is inhibited by formidable economic obstacles.[26]

It should be added that the first edition of this book already mentioned the importance of the cumulative nature of the technological innovations necessary to lead to a real technological revolution. Each of these implies new machine systems, based on different sources of energy. First we had machines produced by handicraft labor, still driven by steam (first technological revolution). Then we had man-operated machines driven by electricity (second technological revolution). The third technological revolution, still unfolding, involves machine-systems that are semiautomatically operated by the massive use of micro-electronics.

Christopher Freeman distinguishes five "Kondratieff waves" (the fifth still under way) in an interesting section that further develops the points we made in this regard. He then concentrates on a thorough analysis of the "third Kondratieff wave," which he calls "the age of steel, electrification and imperialism."[27]

Finally, we should stress a socioeconomic aspect of the problem of technological revolutions, one which serves to link the dynamics of demand to the dynamics of supply. Just taking the third technological revolution, we can say that probably up to 40 percent of the high growth rates of the postwar boom were due to no more than two sectors: housing and automobiles. Not only were billions of units built and sold in these two sectors, they also led to huge sales in other industrial sectors: rubber, ball bearings, batteries, petrol and other fuel, highways, household equipment, paint, glass and so on. For a new expansionary wave to occur, new products must be produced which have the same cumulative dynamic. And that is obviously not the case with color televisions or personal computers. Here we are faced with a basic contradiction of the capitalist growth process: namely, that both a sharp increase in the rate of profit and a huge widening of the market are necessary to bring about a long expansion. Normally, the capitalist way of securing the first condition conflicts with the capitalist way of assuring the second.

Now, to assume that a rising rate of profit will more or less automatically guarantee a parallel expansion of the market for mass consumer goods is as unrealistic as to assume that a massive increase in sales of consumer goods will automatically lead to a rise (not to speak of a long-term rise) in the rate of profit. Only under exceptional circumstances will these two conditions for long-term expansion actually coincide.

A long depression, then, will stimulate the search for new technologies and new products, but it will also inhibit anything beyond the early stages of innovation. So it is not technological innovation *per se* which triggers a new long-term expansion. Only when this expansion has already begun can technological innovations occur on a massive scale. The huge technological rents they generate for the innovating firms then lend momentum to a long-term expansion. Later, of course, when the new technologies and products become more widespread, the technological rents start to be eroded. This happens in spite of efforts by oligopolies to defend them, which include the erection of obstacles to new massive innovations that might "morally depreciate" the huge productive capacities already in place. Hence, the innovation initiative tends to slide toward smaller new firms, although these do not have the means for massive outlays and can operate only as initiators, not as generalizers, of innovations.

We therefore stand by our "accumulation of capital" explanation of the long waves. It is the sum total of factors ultimately offsetting a long-term decline in the rate of profit which are the basic condition of possibility for a new long expansion. Massive technological innovations explain why this movement gathers momentum, not why it occurs.

This whole debate has eminently concrete implications.

Evidently, upturns in the business cycle continue to take place during long depressions, just as periodic crises of overproduction continue to break out during long expansions. But is it a possibility that the present "long depression" will eventually give way to a "soft landing"? In predicting otherwise, we are neither being dogmatic nor engaging in political wishful thinking. We do not exclude such a possibility in principle. We simply identify what is its basic precondition: a massive "system shock" which combines a sharp rise in the rate of profit (induced by an even steeper rise in the rate of surplus value) and a considerable broadening of the market. The latter could only occur, in the present world situation, through total integration of the former USSR and the People's Republic of China into the capitalist world market. The former would necessitate a major defeat of the working class (not necessarily in the form of fascist-like dictatorships) and a no less grave defeat of the "third-world" liberation movements, in both cases at least in all the principal countries.

The first steps in this direction have, to be sure, already occurred, but the end result is far from certain. To assume that the spread of mass unemployment and mass poverty on a world scale could alone produce such outcomes is to discount the potential for mass resistance and its various political crystallizations. In light of what is happening in a number of countries, that is not a realistic hypothesis.[28] So we are drawn back to the problem of the relative autonomy of the class-struggle cycle from long waves in the international capitalist economy as such. From a Marxist point of view, this constitutes a fundamental methodological/theoretical problem, and we only repeat here what we stated at the Brussels colloquium in January 1989.

> To bring the controversy to its vital implication: is the class-struggle cycle mechanically determined by economic forces resulting essentially from levels of employment [i.e., from fluctuations in the reserve army of labor]? Do long-term depressions make crushing defeats of the working class unavoidable? Was Adolf Hitler's victory in 1933 inevitable? Or should one rather

114

say that there is indeed a relative autonomy of long-term class struggle results, a relative desynchronization of the class struggle and the ups and downs of investment, output, employment and income? Can the subjective factor in history...make a decisive difference between victory and defeat of, for example, fascism? . . .

It is undeniable, in the light of empirical evidence, that long-term fluctuations of real wages are not a straightforward function of the ups and downs of the unemployment rate, but a function of a whole series of variables, which I have attempted to analyse elsewhere.

There is an interesting philosophical debate underlying this controversy. Two varieties of determinism confront each other here: mechanical-economic (economistic) rectilinear determinism on the one hand; dialectical parametrical socio-economic determinism on the other hand. I contend that the second version of determinism, which sees two or three possible outcomes for each specific historical crisis – not innumerable ones, for sure, nor ones unrelated to the basic motive forces of a given mode of production, but definitely several ones – corresponds both to Marx's theory and to Marx's analytical practice.[29]

New Issues, New Clarifications

Since the first edition of this book appeared, a number of international scientific colloquia have confirmed the growing interest in the problem of "long waves." Such events took place in June 1985 in Paris, sponsored by the Fernand Braudel Center, Binghamton and the Maison des Sciences de l'Homme; in June 1985 sponsored by the International Institute for Applied Systems Analysis (IIASA); in June 1985 in Weimar (GDR) sponsored by the IIASA; in December 1986 at the Universities of Siena and Florence; in July 1987 at the University of Montpellier, sponsored by the same IIASA and the Fernand Braudel Center; in March 1988 in Novosibirsk (Akademgorodok); and in January 1989 at the Vrije Universiteit Brussels, organized by Kleinknecht, Wallerstein, and myself.

Most of these debates and discussions focused on what David Gordon has called the social conditions of accumulation. In a paper submitted to the Brussels colloquium, Gordon stated that in the first chapter of this book we misinterpreted his views by classifying him among the endogenous school of "long wave" theoreticians. It is possible that our criticism of Gordon was exaggerated. We note, however, that he himself felt the need explicitly to rectify his position on the issue.[1] So, instead of pursuing a superseded polemic, let us conclude that we now largely agree on the importance of the exogenous component ("system shocks") in the causal chain of factors leading from a depressive to an expansionary long wave.

Important new data have underlined the salience of certain trends and events in the long waves of capitalist development.

Let us mention the following in particular: changes in workers' consumption, involving the bundle of what are considered to be "socially necessary" goods and services capable of being purchased by the average wage; changes in the organization of labor at plant level, including in the so-called "service industries"; measurable changes in the intensity and the outcome of current class struggles, especially strikes; changes in the supply of wage labor, including the impact of variations in international migration; connections between the hegemony of a capitalist state in the world market and the capacity of its currency to be accepted worldwide as "general equivalent," to be "as good as gold"; the role of wars, revolutions and counter-revolutions in the rise and decline of such hegemonic powers; the role of the expansion and contraction of credit in the alternation of "long waves"; shifts in "core–periphery" relations and their impact on long waves.

All these areas of clarification enable us to be more precise in analysing both the concept of "social conditions of accumulation" and the "endogenous versus exogenous" debate. Let us first note the contribution by Mauro Galegati from the University of Ancona, which has received too little attention so far.[2] It reintroduces into long wave theory the Keynesian, or neo-Keynesian, dimension of "demand pull" through strong fluctuations of the multiplier. We have fundamental objections to Keynes's explanation of business cycles. But from a Marxist point of view (which considers economic growth [expanded reproduction] as the unity of a process of surplus-value production and a process of surplus value realization, the first by no means guaranteeing the second) a study of the fluctuations of "aggregate demand" during long waves is a necessary and hitherto neglected component of long wave analysis.

Not unrelated to these "aggregate demand" fluctuations is the problem of the level of the "socially necessary wage" during successive long waves. As we have recalled many times, Marx was categorically opposed to any "iron law of wages" theory of the kind adopted by Malthus or Lassalle

117

(and to some extent by Ricardo too), which in the last analysis rests upon demographic considerations. Wages are supposed always to fall to the physiological minimum as a result of variations in the supply of wage laborers due to birth-rate (or child survival) fluctuations. For Marx, by contrast, wages have two components: one physiological, and one "historical" or "social." The former represents the lower limit below which wages cannot fall without threatening to make the working class, and hence capitalism itself, disappear. Similarly, the historical-social component has an upper limit beyond which wages cannot rise without making surplus value, and hence capitalism, disappear. But between the lower and the upper limit wages can and do fluctuate, as a function of what Marx called "the respective powers of the [class] combatants."[3]

We can assume that in general, during the boom phase of the business cycle and during an expansionary long wave, there is greater scope for wage-earners to incorporate new goods and services into the socially recognized average wage. Conversely, during an economic crisis and during a long depression, there is greater scope for capitalists to eliminate a certain number of goods from the average real wage. But these are only possibilities. To what extent they are actually realized, if at all, depends upon a dialectic of the objective and the subjective factors in history, among which the degree of organization, class consciousness and militancy of the two basic classes in bourgeois society, as well as the quality and unity of their leaderships and the character of their historical traditions, play an important role. What Rosa Luxemburg called the civilizing nature of the modern labor movement consists precisely in its tendency to make wage-earners aware of new needs and make them fight for their realization. Marx made the same point in the *Grundrisse*[4] and in the 1861–63 manuscript *Zur Kritik der politischen Ökonomie*. Bebel later expressed it negatively when he spoke of the "damned lack of needs" (*verdammte Bedürfnislosigkeit*) of the workers.

118

To this increase in the mass of goods and services consumed by wage-earners in phases of economic expansion must be added (as Marx again repeatedly stressed) the civilizing effects of the workers' struggle for a shorter working day, including its positive impact on the development of the positive forces. Again, in phases of economic crisis and depression, capital seeks to reverse this trend. But then custom and tradition enter the picture. When working-class families have become accustomed to certain patterns of consumption, and to a certain length of the working day, their resistance to capitalists' attempts to erode previous gains can be very strong, in spite of a deteriorating balance of forces due to mass unemployment. What is currently occurring in the assault on social security provisions well illustrates this tendency.

Capital will try to weaken or break the workers' capacity for resistance by inflating the reserve army of labor and inflicting massive political-social defeats upon the working class. Reorganization of the labor process at plant level is an essential component of the first trend. But this then becomes, together with assaults on real wages, the main cause of mounting class conflicts during the final phase of a depressive long wave.

It is true that the workers often enter a long expansion in a relatively weak position. During the previous depression, their relative class strength has been eroded by long-term mass unemployment and impoverishment, perhaps leading to political defeats. But during the long expansion this strength is gradually rebuilt, thanks to growing employment, better conditions for organization and struggle, and weaker resistance by the employers to wage increases. (Of course, none of these processes develops mechanically; the "subjective factor" always plays a powerful role.)

Conversely, the working class often enters a subsequent depressive wave with greater strength than it entered the expansive wave, a greater capacity to defend itself and fight back (again taking into consideration all the variants of the "subjective factor"). We therefore get a dialectic of uneven

119

and combined development of current economic trends, working-class reactions and economic end results, in which the structural dependence (subordination) of wage labor to capital is combined with the relative autonomy of working-class reactions (struggles). Again this is asymmetrical. Labor cannot prevent capital from reacting to the falling rate of profit through measures which lead to a slump. But the way in which it defends itself will bear upon the capacity of the system to initiate a new long-term boom at labor's expense. There is thus a three-phase movement: initial economic development resulting from the capitalists' decisions; a consequent generation of working-class and intercapitalist reactions and conflicts; ultimate economic developments resulting from interactions between the second and the first. This complex dialectic corresponds to the basic historical fact that capitalist growth is always uneven, disproportionate growth, the outcome of which is not determined in advance.[5]

Francisco Louçã has shed new light on the endogenous vs. exogenous debate, to which he has identified twenty-three contributors.[6] He places the debate within the broader framework of the relationship between scientific discovery and technical progress, going beyond the conclusions that we drew at the beginning of Chapter 2 of this book. We argued there that the relation between scientific progress and long waves can be reduced, in the last analysis, to the role of applied science, in the context of capitalist production and accumulation. But this was in conflict with our own insistence on the relative autonomy of the class-struggle cycle. We agree with Louçã when he rejects the technological-economic paradigm, in favor of the notion of a technological-economic subsystem which, together with socio-institutional changes, essentially accounts for the turn from one long wave to another. Scientific discoveries can add up to constitute a scientific revolution and then trigger a technological revolution. Discussing theories of scientific revolution,[7] Louçã stresses that whereas they mostly start from the premisses of equilibrium theory, economic history confirms the Marxist thesis that capitalism is a system of disequilibrium in which momentary equilibrium is a borderline case. The "endogenous vs. exogenous" debate becomes clearer in the light of this analysis. Thus technological revolutions, as well as heightened class struggle and the relative strength of the working class and the labor movement, are obviously endogenous in long waves. But the actual outcome of class conflicts is not preordained. It is a partially independent variable, and in that precise sense is not endogenous. It is not predictable for the capitalist class. It weighs on its investment decisions and therefore on capital's capacity to launch a new expansionary long wave, regardless of whether discoveries, inventions, and new products are or are not available to unleash a wave of massive technological innovations.[8]

Apart from rationalization (i.e., the stepping up of labor-saving investments), the ups and downs of massive immigration modify the supply/demand ratio for wage labor and thereby the objective relationship of forces between capital and labor.[9] Here too the relationship with long waves has been further elucidated, especially through the work of Lydia Potts.[10] The data she gives show a clear correlation of international migratory waves in all the major capitalist countries throughout the nineteenth and twentieth centuries, with the single exception of Japan. There are strong peaks of international migration during expansionary long waves, whereas there is a relative falling off during long depressions. In the postwar period this correlation with long waves was even more pronounced. In West Germany the number of immigrant workers peaked in 1973 (11.9 percent of the total workforce) and was down to 7.5 percent by 1987. In France the maximum was reached in 1973 and since then has steadily declined.

The following chart displays an impressive correlation for the United States. The fact that the rising immigration trend in the United States does not appear to have been reversed, despite the long depressive wave since the early 1970s, is due to a number of factors.

121

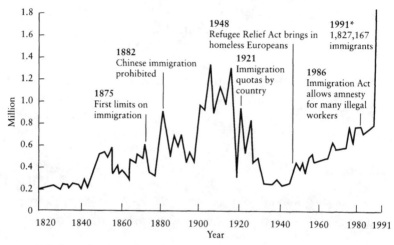

*1991 figure inflated by amnesty in 1986 Act

Figure 12. The major waves of US immigration. Adapted from the *Sunday Times*, August 22, 1993.

First of all, the official figures are misleading with regard to the 1986 Act which grants amnesty to illegal immigrants: that is, they do not reflect an increase in the real level of immigration but only in the number of legally recognized immigrants. It should also be borne in mind that "immigrants" from Puerto Rico are not immigrants at all, as Puerto Rico is a part of the United States. And finally, the "porosity" of the southern frontier of the United States is due not only to the huge wage and welfare differences with Mexico and Central America, but also to the deliberate attempts by North American capitalists to use cheap unprotected immigrant labor as a means of depressing wages in the United States, and to further the "deunionization" of the American working class.

This raises a more general question about international migration under capitalism, a movement of enormous proportions involving more than a hundred million people, sixty million before the early 1920s and more than thirty million after World War II.[11] The traditional literature often lays stress on the immigrants' own initiative in response to wretched conditions in the country of origin, such as the great Irish famine of the 1840s. But that approach only reflects a secondary aspect of the actual historical trend.

Under capitalism, basic economic initiative lies in the hands of capital, not in those of labor. When there is a reduced demand for wage labor in given countries, inward migration will decline, even if poverty and demographic pressure in the countries of emigration continue to rise. What is happening today with immigration from the Maghreb and Black Africa into Western Europe illustrates this fact of capitalist life. Migration, then, essentially answers capital's call and follows the international movements of capital. Indeed, there is a striking fit between such movements and migration flows in the nineteenth and twentieth centuries.[12]

This is why Lydia Potts's assumption that there already exists a world market for wage labor is essentially incorrect. It generalizes what is only an incipient, embryonic tendency. The real worldwide reserve army of labor is enormous: the mass of underemployed, landless laborers and poor peasants in the "third world," as well as the mass of qualitatively underemployed industrial workers there (those who work at a qualitatively lower average productivity of labor), probably add up to more than a billion people. In addition, the industrialized countries themselves have large numbers of housewives and pensioners not currently employed in wage labor who would be quite willing to take up half-time or part-time jobs, were these to be available.

If there did exist a world market for wage labor, this huge mass would increase the supply of labor power in the industrialized and semi-industrialized countries beyond all recognition; this would cause a general trend toward the equalization of wages worldwide, at a level radically lower (let us say four to five times lower) than the average wage in the industrialized countries today. There is absolutely no sign that such a trend is already operating. It might be objected that institutional and political-ideological barriers (racism, sexism, reactions by the unionized "labor aristocracy") prevent this from happening. Potts indeed makes this point. But it is only part of the real process. Behind capital's capacity to manipulate the offer of labor power lies the phenomenon of segmented labor markets, which is fundamentally economic and not purely ideological. This in turn reflects qualitative differences between the mobility of capital, which is nearly unlimited, and the relative immobility of the working class, which has its roots in the very nature of wage labor.[13]

Hence, the capacity of capital to impose all these constraints, and resulting divisions within the modern proletariat, is neither unlimited nor preordained. As in the case of wage fluctuations, it depends at least in part on subjective factors that remain unpredictable for capital. Where there is a certain level of working-class consciousness and a minimum of adequate leadership, the segmentation of labor markets can be partially overcome. Immigrant workers can be increasingly integrated into a more and more united labor force, can even play an organizing role for the "indigenous" working class. There are certainly historical examples of such successful integrations: Jewish workers in Amsterdam, New York or Thessaloniki, the Jewish Bund in parts of Russian Poland, Italian workers in Belgium and Switzerland, Italian and Spanish workers in other European countries. It has to be recognized, of course, that for the last 150 years these are the exceptions rather than the rule. But the conclusion still stands. Capital does not have in advance an unrestricted capacity to *impose* segmented labor markets, and thus to secure huge increases in the rate of surplus value that decisively contribute to a rise in the rate of profit and help to trigger a new expansionary long wave. The degree of working-class resistance is largely unpredictable for capital. It is a partially independent variable.

Elmar Altvater has drawn attention to the quite different degrees of success that capital achieves in its attempts to impose a "dual society," according to the institutional context in which the working class and the labor movement are historically placed.[14] He identifies four distinct situations: continuing relative strength of trade unions, as in the "welfare states" of Western Europe; relative weakness or persistent decline of unions (United States); a brutal and successful breaking of union power by the government (Britain); a government drive to "deregulate" the labor market in the absence of strong independent unions, with measures of social protection either accorded or withheld according to the economic policy orientation and the degree of mass resistance (Eastern Europe and the former USSR). He could have added a fifth category: namely, countries like India where a huge reserve army of labor makes the trade union movement chronically weak

Altvater's typology clearly confirms the different degrees of working-class resistance to the attempted imposition of large increases in the rate of surplus value. He also stresses new forms of segmentation of the labor market: internationally, by transfers to the "third world" of less skilled and high-polluting jobs; in the West, a (modest) increase in self-employment made possible by "micro-electronics", and the encouragement of immigration by highly skilled workers from Eastern Europe, as opposed to low-skilled immigrants.

Altvater assumes, however, that moves toward worldwide "regulation," with the emergence of new social conditions of accumulation, are somehow automatically successful. This seriously underestimates the various degrees of workers' resistance depending upon a number of political-ideological (subjective) factors. Eric Tucker, for example, makes the following point:

> Ontario's experience is instructive. It showed that a concerted campaign by workers to politicize the problem of unsafe and unhealthy workplaces can put pressure on the state to exercise its regulatory powers more forcefully. When this is accompanied by the election of a government which feels itself to be at least somewhat dependent on workers' votes, a tougher approach to enforcement may be implemented.[15]

125

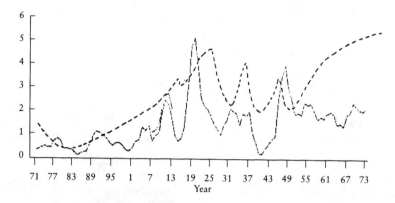

Figure 13. Class Struggles (1871–1973).

This analysis strengthens our thesis of a long-term class-struggle cycle, which is one of this book's main new contributions to long wave theory. In Figure 3 (p. 39 this volume) I projected a general trend of European class struggle, derived from general historical knowledge but uncorroborated by empirical data. Beverly Silver has drawn up a curve based on newspaper reports of major workers' struggles, which dovetails quite closely with my own projected curve. If there is a discrepancy, it is mainly due to the fact that Spain (the country where class explosions peaked several times in the twentieth century) is absent from Silver's data.[16] In the following historical scale of class struggles from 1871 to 1973, the unbroken line is Silver's and the dotted one is taken from the first edition of this book.

At the Brussels symposium in 1989 Giorgio Gattei presented statistics on the number of strike days in Britain, Germany, France, the United States, and Italy, which show peaks in 1893, 1905–06 (revolution in Russia!), 1911–13 (1913 having the absolute maximum before World War I), 1919–21 (Russian and German revolutions, big strike wave in Northern Italy), 1926 (British General Strike). The statistics are somewhat flawed because they leave out France 1936–45, Spain 1912–37 and Germany 1933–48 (after 1945 there was an important strike wave in Germany). Gattei summarizes his findings in the following table:[17]

Turning Point of the Long Cycles	Maxima of Activity (Strikes & Disputes)
1844–51	1847–49
1866–75	1868–73
1892–96	1893
1913–20	1919–21
1939–48	1946–49
1967–74	1968

Ernesto Screpanti, in the following graph, correlates essentially the same strike data with the long waves of the capitalist economy.[18] Beyond this statistical corroboration of long class-struggle cycles, with peaks and troughs roughly alternating over fifty years each, Screpanti had previously

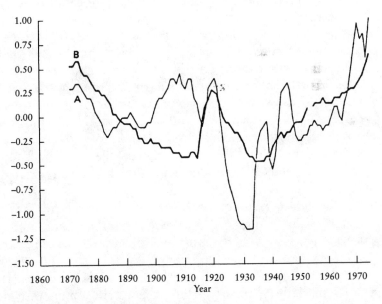

Figure 14. Long cycles in strike activity.

127

attempted a most subtle explanation of the recurrent peaks of international working-class explosions in relation to long waves of capitalist development.[19] This interconnection is structured around the readiness of capitalists to engage in large-scale investment, according to their awareness and fears of workers' militancy and restiveness. And this is in turn bound up with waves of working-class achievement and frustration, related to the effects of long expansions and long depressions upon the class relationship of forces and the level of class consciousness.

There are a number of interesting and persuasive elements in this analysis. But it suffers simultaneously from an excessively "voluntarist" and an excessively fatalistic bias. Thus, the willingness of capital to launch a massive wave of investment at the end of a long depression is not adequately related to a strong surge in the rate of profit. The degree of resistance (frustration) of the working class is not adequately related to employers' attempts to introduce a radical change in the organization of labor, which is one of the ways for capital to drive up the rate of surplus value and thereby the rate of profit. Nor is there sufficient understanding of the uncertain, unpredictable outcome of these trials of strength and their connection with the relative power and weakness of the working class (the labor movement) during the previous 25-year period. At the same time, Screpanti tries to explain the successive waves of workers' militancy and class explosions essentially as spontaneous impulses and movements, thereby reducing the role of organizations and the clash of leaderships. This leads him to identify worldwide patterns which do not correspond to the historical reality.

Why did the revolution of 1848 not extend to Britain? Why did the Commune of 1871 occur in Paris and not in Germany? Why was the Russian Revolution victorious and the German Revolution defeated? Why did the German labor movement capitulate before Hitler in 1933 and the Austrian and especially Spanish working classes rise up against fascism in 1934–36? Why has there never been a nationwide general strike in the United States? Why did the Argentine working class, which held a large number of general strikes, never challenge the political power of the bourgeoisie, whereas the Brazilian working class, with much less strike experience, at least appears to be initiating such a challenge? Are these differences insignificant? Were the defeats inevitable? We believe that our explanation of the relatively autonomous class-struggle cycle, while certainly more simple than Screpanti's, better corresponds to what really happened in history as well as being theoretically more coherent. It would certainly profit greatly from incorporating some of Screpanti's contributions.

The relationship between the relatively autonomous class-struggle cycle and long waves of capitalist development is rooted in, among other things, the very nature of the bourgeoisie and the wage-earners as social classes. In the capitalist mode of production, the bourgeoisie is perfectly capable of laying off workers and closing down factories on a large scale, if this corresponds to its current preoccupations and interests. The wage-earning class could prevent this only by directly challenging the power of capital nationwide. There is no historical example of this happening during a severe economic crisis, although it might have developed in Germany in 1923 and again in the early 1930s if the rise of fascism had been successfully reversed. Nevertheless, in the latter phase of a crisis and during a long depression, capital is not able mechanically to impose on a restive working class policies which would entail that the price of the crisis is paid by the workers. Capital has total power over plants and machines. It does not have total power over living labor.

In a similar vein to Screpanti's, some authors have even ventured to correlate "war cycles" with long waves. Again, they offer interesting material, but their conclusions are too mechanistic. What is important to stress, however, even more than we did in the first edition of this book, is that the existence (or absence) of a hegemonic power on the world market is of great importance for the expansion of large-scale credit in the international capitalist economy. There can be no doubt that US capitalism has lost its absolute hegemony on the world market. This can be seen clearly from the following table.

Table 6.1. US production as a percentage of production of other countries

	1970	1975	1980	1986	1987
Japan	495	317	254	214	188
W. Germany	547	371	330	469	401
EC	158	113	93	131	104
Japan & EC	113	77	64	77	67

This has major implications for the capacity of the system to postpone the day of reckoning by means of inflation.[20] As indicated above, a nonhegemonic power cannot in the long run impose on its competitors and on individual capitalists its own depreciated paper currency as general equivalent, by essentially military-political means. If the decline of the dollar has not yet turned into a free fall, it is because US imperialism, while losing its lead in labor productivity over certain West European countries and Japan, maintains and even increases this superiority compared with "third-world" and former Eastern bloc countries. These then suffer what Pierre Salama has tellingly called a "dollarization" of their economies.

Throughout the history of modern capitalism, a growing conflict has arisen between the tendency of capital to operate on a world scale and its structuring, for reasons of self-defence, as national capital. There is a tendency for this conflict to become relatively milder during long expansionary waves and relatively sharper during long depressions.

Contemporary imperialism was born as a result of the long 1873–93 depression, with its protectionist and "beggar-thy-neighbour" impetus, and its violent wars of colonial conquest. During the long expansionary wave that followed in 1893–1913 (when all powers profited, albeit in different degrees, from the growth in world trade) inter-imperialist

130

rivalry continued to increase. At first this took on a more peaceful aspect: no major wars occurred, with the exception of the one between Russia and Japan. But the arms drive swiftly gathered pace and, as the expansionary forces spent themselves, a major war became likely. Its outbreak just after the big economic crisis of 1913 was not a mere coincidence.

During the long depression of 1913–40(48), the breakup of the world market among predominantly national capitalist powers – what Bukharin called "state capitalist trusts"[21] – became a defining feature of the world situation. Internationalization of capital seemed to be on the retreat. It may be argued, of course, that these were just stepping stones toward international expansionism, which was itself a springboard for the conquest of world hegemony, as reflected by US imperialism in Latin America, German imperialism in Central and Eastern Europe, British imperialism in the Middle East, Japanese imperialism in China and South Asia. But the fundamental trend was one of fragmentation, not of further unification of the world market.[22]

From 1949 on, the tendency was increasingly reversed. This process was certainly not unrelated to the emergence of US imperialism as the hegemonic power in the world economy, but the basic cause lay deeper. It corresponded to the growing internationalization of the productive forces, the growing internationalization of "functioning" capital, the emergence of the multinational (transnational) corporation as the predominant capitalist form on the world market.[23]

These multinational corporations became more and more autonomous of even the most powerful states. One major consequence of this weakness of the bourgeois state vis-à-vis "functioning capital" is the growing privatization of money, a most striking feature of the present depressive long wave. Credit money creation increasingly takes place through speculative operations which no state body controls, whose precise extent is not even known.[24] The bourgeoisie continues to need state power. But under conditions where "functioning capital" is predominantly internationalized, the only adequate form of state power would be a world state, which is precisely what cannot be realized under capitalism, for both economic and social-political reasons.

The contradictions of inter-imperialist competition and the absence of a single hegemonic power are illustrated by what is occurring in the field of electronics. Japan and South Korea have gained a significant advance *vis-à-vis* the USA in many of the subfields of electronics. But with regard to the diffusion of personal computers and users of cable television, the USA are far in advance of Japan as is shown by the following table.

Table 6.2. The advance of the USA (1993 figures)

Equipment and networks	Japan	USA
Personal computers per 100 inhabitants	5.7	15.2
Personal computers per 100 employees	10	42
Personal computers linked to local networks (%)	9%	52%
Personal computers linked to Internet	39,000	1,180,000
Cable TV companies	149	11,075
Cable TV subscribers (millions)	1 (3% of homes)	57 (60% of homes)

Le Monde Diplomatique, February 1995

This is not unrelated to the specific form of Japanese capitalism's semi-authoritarian methods of control over the Japanese people, as stressed and denounced by Associate Professor Eisshi Katsura, of Tokyo University of Art and Design (ibidem).

More in general, Karel van Wolferen (*The Enigma of Japanese Power*, Vintage Books, New York 1990) argues that the outstanding successes of the Japanese economy, its export drive, its huge balance of payments surplus, its "funding" of the US deficits, has been largely due to government orientation. Therefore "the bubble [of skyrocketing land and stock prices] does not burst" (p. 399). But won't it in the future?

In fact, of the three big capitalist power blocks, the USA,

Japan, and Germany, Japan seems the most vulnerable. And this, as we have said before, is not unrelated to the specific forms of bourgeois rule in that country, the specific ways in which it tries to extract (impose) consensus in society, including inside the ruling class itself.

In the light of this consideration, an important addition has to be made to the line of reasoning which I defend in this book with regard to the importance of the subjective factor in history, more precisely the concrete dialectic of the objective and the subjective factors in history.

When we speak about the uncertain outcome of class struggles during a long depressive wave, we have to examine not only the situation of the wage-earning class but also that of the ruling class. While it is clear that the relative strength of the working class is weakened by rising unemployment in the depression, we stressed repeatedly that this weakening is only relative. The wage earners keep a great potential of resistance, accumulated during the previous expansive long wave.

Now precisely for that reason, the capitalist class is divided during a phase of the depression on the strategy to follow regarding the ways and means of imposing on the wage earners the burden of the restoration of the rate of profit through a radical increase in the rate of surplus value (the rate of exploitation). Its hesitations are due to the fact that if it "goes too far" it might provoke very large "fight back" reactions by the toilers. What is happening now in the USA, Britain, France, Spain, and Italy confirms this diagnosis.

German and Spanish capitalists did not unanimously opt in favor of fascism in 1933 and 1936 – far from it. In Germany they hesitated on a course of trying to crush immediately the labor movement even after Hitler became chancellor. They were afraid of civil war – as did actually occur in Spain, where they miscalculated gravely and nearly lost. If they did win after all in Spain, this was due to the weakness of the "subjective factor" on the side of the workers, inadequacy of revolutionary consciousness, and leadership not predetermined ("overdetermined") by economic conditions.

Economically, competition continues to operate within the framework of internationalized capital, as a result of the persistence of private property (many capitals). Politically, the relative efficiency of state power as a means of political-social defense of bourgeois rule still largely depends upon the legitimacy of nation-states, while emerging transnational state bodies suffer from a lack of anything really comparable. Because there is no bourgeois world state and money needs the underpinning of a state,[25] there is no real world money.[26] The growing privatization of money therefore implies growing international monetary disorder. And such disorder becomes an important additional obstacle preventing an end to the current long depression.

One of the general features of any long depressive wave is the progressive speeding-up of capital depreciation. As technological innovations become "popularized," the commodities in which they are embodied become cheaper. A good example is that of computers, and especially of their microchip and semi-conductor components. A microcomputer today costs 10,000 times less than the first ENIAC computer, has the capacity to compute 20 times faster, and occupies only 1/30,000th of the space. Integrated circuits seem to double in complexity with every year that passes. In 1976–78 each circuit contained more than 262,000 "bits." The cost of one "bit" stored in memory was reduced by 35 percent per year in the 1970s.[27]

But then comes the hitch. Who is going to buy 25 percent more chips, integrated circuits or semi-conductors each year? Already in 1960, five billion transistors were being produced. Will there be a saleable output of five billion transistors a year to keep up with the reduction in production costs? And if this does not happen, technological rents disappear and even average profits are doomed to decline.[28]

So what had to happen did happen. In 1984 IBM made after-tax profits of almost $7 billion: no other company in the world has ever made as much. In 1992 IBM lost $5 billion, more than any other company ever did in the world. The figure either way is larger than the total GDP of more than ten of the hundred major countries in the world.[29]

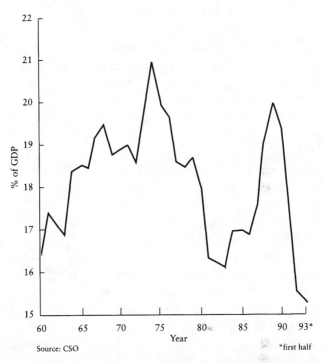

Figure 15. UK capital expenditure. Adapted from the *Sunday Times*, August 29, 1993.

More precisely, and with less extrapolation, Professor Walter Kunerth, executive vice-president of Siemens, states: "The higher the level of technology, the more the need for capital, the fewer the players and the greater the need for a big market." One might add: and the lower the profits. Another expert used a striking image: if Rolls Royce had achieved the same productivity gains as the television industry, a Rolls would cost the same today as a bicycle.[30] There you have in a nutshell the main "laws of motion" of capitalism as laid bare by Karl Marx.[31]

Robots are another example of this basic contradiction. When they started to be produced, overenthusiastic observers spoke about a withering away of human labor. Each robot used in industry replaces on average two jobs, with one overseer remaining for every four to five machines.[32] That would really be the "post-industrial society," but also the post-market society, as Marx already predicted in the *Grundrisse* 140 years ago. Unfortunately for the diehards of market economy, robots do not buy goods and services. But they do produce a mountain of increasingly unsaleable goods.[33]

Be this as it may, all the stories about "robots and the disappearance of human labor" turned out to be science fiction. We are not living in the age of full automation. We are still living in the age of semiautomation. Already in 1983 Stanley Polcyn predicted that in the early 1990s only 40,000 robots would be sold annually, for a total of no more than $2 billion.[34] And now there has appeared an overproduction of robots and overcapacity of the robot-producing industry.[35] All this means that technological rents disappear, and that large masses of commodity capital and fixed capital lose part of their value. Depreciation of capital entails relative shortage of available capital, which makes massive investment in new technologies and new products more difficult.[36]

At first sight, this conclusion contradicts one of the key features of the present long depression. How can one talk of devalorization of capital in a world awash with paper money, under conditions of declining inflation? But the paradox is only apparent. The great bulk of "floating" paper money is in the hands of those sectors of the capitalist class who basically operate in speculation (real estate, stock market or currency speculation) and not in the field of surplus value production. But the enormous mass of interest they receive is subtracted from the total of currently produced surplus value. Therefore, the fraction of that surplus-value available for current productive investment declines, as does expanded reproduction (growth) of the economy as a whole. The average rate of profit remains relatively depressed. The end of the long depression is not in sight.

Let us illustrate this phenomenon by a nearly unbelievable figure. According to the *Financial Times* of March 21, 1994, the notional value of futures contracts traded on all world exchanges has reached a total of $14 trillion a year: $14,000,000,000,000! Of course, the same speculators may well use the same advances in several successive operations, so that the actual annual outlay in futures trading may be more like $14 trillion divided by five or ten. But even that is a staggering figure if one considers that according to the Chase Manhattan Bank, total privately owned capital excluding real estate and housing amounted worldwide in 1993 to $10 trillion.

To conclude, then, the sum of all the factors discussed in this chapter points to the basic weakness of the theory of (self-)regulation of contemporary capitalism. To be sure, capitalism means bourgeois power in most fields of social activity. And this implies the capacity of capital to correlate new patterns of productive investment (accelerated technological research and innovation), new forms of labor organization, new patterns of workers' consumption, and new variants of social ideas and illusions, including within important sectors of the working class (consumerism, neo-reformism, "consensus politics", etc.). But this (self-)regulating capacity is not unlimited. It faces two major obstacles: capitalist competition and the workers' capacity for resistance. These obstacles cannot be easily overcome. They certainly cannot be overcome automatically.

The very nature of a long depression makes any attempt in that direction not just difficult but unrealistic. If long periods of prosperity create more favorable conditions for compromise and "consensus," long periods of depression favor conflicts in which all contenders refuse to make important concessions. Not successful regulation but growing contradictions and strife tend to prevail.

So there will be no "soft landing" from the long depression, only business cycle upturns followed by new recessions, with a steady increase in unemployment and long-term average rates of growth much lower than those of the "postwar boom."

Notes

Chapter 1

1. See Mandel, *Late Capitalism* (London, 1975), Chapter 4, for a detailed discussion of these contributions, as well as of the whole long waves controversy of the last eighty years.

2. An excellent bibliographical survey of the long waves literature and controversy is offered by Kenneth Barr, "Long Waves: A Selective Annotated Bibliography," *Review* (Binghamton) 2(1979):675. The only notable omissions are two German works: Hans Rosenberg, *Grosse Depression und Bismarckzeit* (Berlin, 1967), which has an extensive bibliography, and Gerhard Mensch, *Das technologische Patt* (Frankfurt am Main, 1975).

3. W. W. Rostow, *The World Economy, History and Prospects* (Austin, 1978).

4. Angus Maddison, "Phases of Capitalist Development," *Banca Nazionale del Lavoro Quarterly Review* (June 1977), p. 103. This is an extended version of a paper presented at the 1977 meeting of the World Congress of Economists in Tokyo.

5. Jay Forrester in *Fortune* magazine, January 16, 1978, issue. This interview is a summary of a more extensive treatment of the long waves problem by Forrester, "Business Structure, Economic Cycles and National Policy," *Futures* (1976): 195–214

6. On this issue, see the bibliography cited in Note 2: Barr, *Review* 2(1979):675. Andre Gunder Frank strongly defends the idea that an upswing long wave started around 1789.

7. They are especially strong in the Cassel-Kitchin-Woytinski tradition and in the French school based on the work of François Simiand.

8. Elmar Altvater, Jürgen Hoffmann, and Willi Semmler, *Vom Wirtschaftswunder zur Wirtschaftskrise* (Berlin, 1979), pp. 25–26.

9. See Robert Rowthorn, *New Left Review* (1976):59, and Erik Olin Wright, *Class, Crisis and the State* (London, 1978), p. 164. In

139

addition, I would make the modest claim of not belonging among those who appear lucid only with hindsight. I predicted the turn from the expansionist long wave to the depressive long wave before it took place ["The Economics of Neo-Capitalism," *The Socialist Register* (1964:56)] and situated the probable turning point rather correctly for the late 1960s.

10. One recent variant is based on the so-called Okiskio theorem, which postulates that since no entrepreneur will introduce a new technology that does not maintain or increase the profit rate, what is true for every single firm must also be true for the economy as a whole. This theorem obviously misunderstands the very nature of capitalism (i.e., private production and thus unavoidable competition), thereby forgetting that economic agents, including entrepreneurs, cannot correctly foresee the objective aggregate outcome of their decisions, which might be the opposite of what they intend to achieve. It abstracts from the very nature of capitalist competition. What is good for certain firms is not necessarily true for all of them. For a good answer to the Okiskio theorem, see Anwar Shaikh, *Cambridge Journal of Economics* (1978).

11. The Hungarian Marxist P. Erdös, "A Contribution to the Interrelation between the Theory of Reproduction and That of Business Fluctuations," *For the Progress of Marxist Economics* (Budapest, 1967), has criticized, from a Marxist point of view, the *ex ante* profit concept as a decisive determinant in business cycles, insisting on its psychological (i.e., subjective) character. However, it is not difficult to show that these *ex ante* profit expectations that determine investment decisions are not subjective at all, but are functions of objective factors, among them the *ex post* profits of the previous period (year, reproduction cycle, etc.), market trends, market provisions, etc.

12. For a summary and a large anthology of that controversy, see L. Colletti and C. Napoleoni (editors), *Il Futuro del Capitalismo – Crollo o Sviluppo?* (Bari, 1970).

13. We have dealt with that subject, inter alia, in *Late Capitalism* (London, 1975), pp. 149–58, and in our introduction to Volume I of *Capital* (Harmondsworth, Middlesex, 1976).

14. See Karl Marx (e.g., on the fluctuations of real wages during periods of boom), *Capital*, Chapter 32; *Marx-Engels-Werke* (Berlin, 1969), Volume 25, pp. 529–30, 876ff.

15. Christian Sautter, "Phases et Formes structurelles du

NOTES

capitalisme japonais,' *Quatre Économies Dominantes sur Longue Période*, Institut National de la Statistique et des Etudes Economiques, Paris, 1978, pp. 178–179. The figures are based on calculations in Ohkawa-Rosovsy, *Japanese Economic Growth* (Stanford, 1978), and C. Sautter, *Le Ralentissement de la Croissance au Japon et en France d'ici 1980* (Paris, 1978).

16. Sidney Homer, *A History of Interest Rates*, 2nd edition (New Brunswick, 1977). For long-term yields in Britain, see pp. 505 and 195–6; for long-term yields in the United States and Switzerland, see p. 505. For short-term yields, see p. 513. The data on France are from Robert Marjolin, *Prix, Monnaie, et Production. Essai sur les mouvements économiques de longue durée* (Paris, 1941), p. 207.

17. Trotsky was the first to set the Marxist theory of long periods (phases, waves) of development in the capitalist economy in opposition to the Kondratieff concept of mechanical cycles. See Leon Trotsky, "O krivoi kapitalisticheskovo razvitiya" (On the Curve of Capitalist Development), *Viestnik sotsialisticheskoi Akademii*, No. 4, April-June 1923; English translation in *Fourth International*, May 1941.

18. Richard Day, *New Left Review* (1976):67, thought that we had overlooked Trotsky's attack on Kondratieff's fundamental thesis that capitalism can somehow reestablish its equilibrium more or less automatically after that equilibrium has been broken in a long wave with depressive undertone. This is not true. In *Late Capitalism* we shared Trotsky's view that there is no automatic inner logic of capitalism that can lead from a depressive long wave to an expansive long wave. Outside factors ("system-shocks," to quote Angus Maddison) are indispensable for that purpose. That we are in no sense "neo-harmonicists," believing in the capitalist system's capacity to reestablish equilibrium automatically, should be clear to any reader of *Late Capitalism*, in which such views as expounded by Hilferding and Bukharin are severely criticized.

19. Angus Maddison (as cited in Note 4, p. 120) also concluded that "he move from one phase to another is caused by system-shocks. These shocks may well be due to a predictable breakdown of some basic characteristic of a previous phase, but the timing of the change is usually governed by exogenous or accidental events which are not predictable." This is true for the turning point from a stagnating long wave to an expansive long wave. It is not true for the turning point from an expansive long wave to a stagnating one.

20. In an interesting study published by the Ecole Nationale Supérieure de Techniques Avancées (ENSTA, No. 37, 1974), F. Hoffherr and R. Leruste empirically demonstrated a close correlation between fluctuations in the rate of profit (as calculated by them, which obviously differs from the Marxist concept of the rate of profit, but not sufficiently to make the correlation meaningless from a Marxist point of view) and economic growth for West Germany, Britain, and France in the 1950s and 1960s.

21. We can distinguish two phases in each expansive long wave, a first one in which "extensive" industrialization prevails, precisely because of the relative low level of wages, and a second one in which, as a result of the drying up of the industrial reserve army of labor (the realization of "full employment"), there is a definite premium on the production of relative surplus value (i.e., on the increase in productivity of labor in the consumer-goods sector). It is obviously during this second subphase that all the inner contradictions of the capitalist system come steadily to the fore, preparing the unavoidable turning point toward a long wave with depressive trend.

22. One must take into consideration additional factors of international migration. In the second half of the nineteenth century, migration of surplus labor from European countries in the process of industrialization to North America far outweighed migration within Europe, thereby creating a secular decline of the industrial reserve army in Western and Central Europe, which led to conditions favorable for the emergence of a mass labor movement in the 1880s and 1890s. Conversely, the drying up of manpower reserves inside Western Europe in the 1960s led to massive migration toward these industrialized countries from the Mediterranean countries, including North Africa and Turkey, from the West Indies, India, and Pakistan, and even from South Korea (e.g., hospital personnel in West Germany). Similar movements occurred in the United States (massive immigration from Puerto Rico, Mexico, and Central America) during the postwar boom and in the Middle East starting in the 1960s and increasing after the 1973 rise in oil prices (influx of supplementary manpower into Kuwait, Saudi Arabia, the Persian Gulf states, etc., not only of Palestinians, Egyptians, and Pakistanis but even South Korean laborers).

23. W. Woytinski, "Das Rätsel der langen Wellen," *Schmollers Jahrbuch* 55(1931).

24. It is clear that during an expansionist long wave the basic laws of motion of capitalism operate in a double sense. Once the upswing has started, through a strong increase in the rate of profit, the technological revolution "feeds on itself" (i.e., it allows an above-average rate of growth in department I producing equipment and an above-average rate of productive investment for a whole period). In the opposite sense, once this above-average rate of development in department I passes a certain threshold, both the growth in the organic composition of capital and the effects of the technological revolution on the productive capacity of department II inexorably work toward the combination of a declining rate of profit and a realization crisis.

25. See, in addition to the article by Day (as cited in Note 18), Marcel van der Linden, *Vrij Nederland Kleurkatern* (19):20, and Chris Harman, *International Socialism* (1978):79.

26. This thesis was violently challenged by various Marxist authors like Martin Nicolaus and Christian Palloix. Since then, events have arbitrated the controversy.

27. "The explanation of this book is that the 1929 depression was so wide, so deep and so long because the international economic system was rendered unstable by British inability and US unwillingness to assume for stabilizing it in three particulars: (a) maintaining a relatively open market for distress goods; (b) providing countercyclical long-term lending; (c) discounting in crisis. . . . The world economic system was unstable unless some country stabilized it, as Britain had done in the 19th century and up to 1913. In 1929, the British couldn't and the US wouldn't." Charles P. Kindleberger, *The World in Depression 1929–1939*, pp. 291–2. London, 1973.

28. There are innumerable corroborations of this. A former cabinet minister in France, Mr Jeanneney, recently published a book in defense of "moderate protectionism." The German liberal weekly *Die Zeit* published in its November 17, 1978, issue a review of an international symposium on the subject, organized by Sperry Rand in November 1978 near Nice, in which, besides politicians (and prominent representatives of the Trilateral Commission) and leading technocrats of international institutions, many world-renowned businessmen and bankers participated. The review carries an eloquent title: "Nobody Believes Any More in Free Trade." See also the pamphlet "The Rise in Protectionism" published in 1978 by the

International Monetary Fund, and the articles of similar content in the September 1978 issue of the trimestral publication of that fund, "Finances and Development."

29. Gustav Cassel, *The Theory of Social Economy* (New York, 1924), pp. 441ff. Also see Woytinski (as cited in Note 23) and Robert Marjolin, Prix, *Monnaie et Production* (Paris, 1941). It should be recalled that Kautsky, in "Die Wandlungen der Goldproduktion und der wechselnde Charakter der Teuerung" (supplement to *Die Neue Zeit*, No. 16, January 24, 1913), had insisted on the fact that major gold discoveries in the nineteenth century had occurred before upswings, thereby stimulating investments.

30. Leo Katzen, *Gold and the South African Economy* (Cape Town/Amsterdam, 1964), p. 233. This hypothesis is based on the fact that during depressions, prices (expressed in gold currencies) fall. Thereby, the terms of trade of gold as against all other commodities (or between gold-exporting countries and all other countries) rise, the rate of profit in gold mining likewise rises, capital is attracted to gold mining, and gold production goes up.

31. "In the 19th century, changes in the supply of gold were largely due to fortuitous discoveries of new ore resources and their exhaustion. Cost factors were relatively unimportant, as the base capital equipment was often little more than a shallow pan or machinery of the simplest kind. . . . For the last 50 to 60 years, accident has ceased to play a very big part in changes in the supply of gold. Gold mining has come to be undertaken by very large units, mining at deep levels with expensive capital equipment. Improved techniques have reduced the risk factor in gold mining and prospecting. In short, it has become an industry which is just as sensitive to costs and price as any other industry." Katzen (as cited in Note 30), p. 9.

32. This applies not only to the amplitude of capital investment in gold mining but also to its participation in the equalization of the rate of profit of imperialist capital exports. In that respect, see S. Herbert Frankel, *Investment and the Return on Equity Capital in the South African Gold-Mining Industry 1887–1965* (Cambridge, Mass., 1967).

33. This implies, of course, two simultaneous factors: a tremendous increase in differential rent for the richer mines and the possibility of reopening many poor mines, not only in South Africa but also in the United States. See *The New York Times*, July 28, 1979, which speaks of a "second [gold] rush out West" and indi-

cates that at the current level of the "price of gold," "it pays to move five tons of rock to obtain an ounce of gold."

34. It is interesting to note that the search for gold in the Transvaal started in the early 1850s through the late 1860s and does not seem to have been accelerated by any chronic "scarcity of gold" during the long depression of 1873–93.

35. It would be a revealing story to connect the long-term trend in the value of gold (and the value of all other commodities expressed in gold, i.e., the secular price trend) to the hunger wages paid to South African black miners (i.e., to all the trappings of racism and the apartheid regime that make these low wages and thereby the relatively low production costs of South African gold possible). According to Katzen, working costs per ton milled in South African gold mines remained practically stable for more than forty years, with only minor fluctuations. They stood at 25/9 sh. per ton in 1902 and at 25/7 sh. per ton in 1946 (there were successive declines in the pre-World War I period, rises between 1916 and 1922, a new decline between 1921 and 1936, and a new rise after 1936, which by 1946 reached the 1902 level again) (Katzen, as cited in Note 30, pp. 18–19). Wage costs represent more or less half of total costs. Wages for black workers are exactly 10 percent of those for white employees. Between 1914 and 1920, they rose by only 10 percent, whereas the cost of living rose by 55 percent. Between 1940 and 1950, they rose by 48.7 percent, as compared with a rise in retail prices of 65 percent. They rose a further 36 percent between 1950 and 1961, but even that rise barely kept pace with the rise in retail prices over the same period (Katzen, Note 30, pp. 22–23). Black workers' real wages were probably lower in the middle 1960s than at the beginning of the century! According to Francis Wilson, *Labour in the South African Mines, 1911–1969* (Cambridge, 1972), real wages stood at index 109 in 1969, as compared with index 111 in 1911. Katzen concluded: "It is clear that any substantial narrowing of the gap between white and African miners' wages would make an enormous difference to mining costs. If we take the year 1930, for example, and assume that African miners were suddenly to have received the same wages as white miners, working costs for that year instead of being £31 million would have risen to approximately £100 million, i.e., more than twice the value of the gold produced in that year." Katzen, Note 30, p. 22.

36. G. G. Matyushin, *Problems of Credit-Money under Capitalism* (Moscow, 1977).

Chapter 2

1. From the growing literature on the subject, let us cite the following: J. D. Bernal, *Science in History* (London, 1969); S. Lilley, "Social Aspects of the History of Science," *Archives Internationales d'Histoire des Sciences*, 28(1949):376; Thomas S. Kuhn, *The Structure of Scientific Revolutions* (London, 1964); *Die Wissenschaft von der Wissenschaft* (by a collective of the Leipzig Karl Marx University) (Leipzig, 1968); Benjamin Coriat, *Science, Technique et Capital* (Paris, 1976); Pierre Papon, *Le Pouvoir et la Science en France* (Paris, 1979); Robert B. Lindsay, *The Role of Science in Civilization* (London, 1963); J. Agassi, *Towards a Historiography of Science* (The Hague, 1963); D. Gabor, *Innovations: Scientific, Technological and Social* (Harmondsworth Middlesex, 1970); Peter Weingart Hrsgb., *Wissenschaftliche Entwicklung als sozialer Prozess* (Frankfurt, 1972); Peter Bulthaup, *Zur gesellschaftlichen Funktion der Naturwissenschaften* (Frankfurt, 1973); Hans-Jörg Sandkühler Hrsgb., *Marxistische Wissenschaftstheorie* (Frankfurt, 1975).

2. Marx used the category of "general labor" explicitly in relation to scientific labor. *Capital* (Berlin, 1969), Volume 3.

3. Karl Marx, *Grundrisse* (Harmondsworth, Middlesex, 1975), pp. 703–4.

4. E. Mandel, *Late Capitalism* (London, 1975), pp. 249–59. See also Harry Braverman, *Labor and Monopoly Capital* (New York, 1974), pp. 157–66.

5. Arthur Clegg, "Craftsmen and the Origin of Science," *Science and Society* 43(1979):187.

6. Harry Braverman (as cited in Note 4, pp. 132–4); David Landes, *Prometheus Unbound* (Cambridge, 1970), pp. 62–3.

7. This was certainly a common feature of the 1920s and of the 1970s, especially after the 1974–5 recession. On the first rationalization wave, see Lyndall Urwick, *The Meaning of Rationalization* (London, 1929), as well as Otto Bauer *Rationalisierung und Fehlrationalisierung* (Vienna, 1931).

8. Gerhard Mensch, *Das technologische Patt* (Frankfurt am Main, 1975), pp. 142–5.

9. To extend the historical analogy backward, let us point out

that, according to David Landes (as cited in Note 6), p. 237, by the last quarter of the nineteenth century "the exhaustion of the technological possibilities of the Industrial Revolution" had set in. Investment did not involve large-scale technological innovations, at least in the earlier industrialized countries. On this subject, see H. Rosenberg, *Grosse Depression und Bismarckzeit* (Berlin, 1967).

10. Jacob Schmookler, "Economic Sources of Inventive Activity," *Journal of Economic History* 22(1962):1.

11. W. Rupert Maclaurin, "The Sequence from Invention to Innovation and Its Relation to Economic Growth," *Quarterly Journal of Economics* 67(1953):96.

12. Ibid., p. 108.

13. George Ray, "Innovation in the Long Cycle," *Lloyds Bank Review*, January 1980, p. 21, correctly noted: "From the point of view of its impact on the economy, it is not the basic innovation but its *diffusion* across industry or the economy, and the *speed* of this diffusion, that matters. Only the widely-based rapid diffusion of some major innovations can be assumed to play any part in triggering off the Kondratiev – or any other – long-term upswing."

14. See Robert Blauner, *Alienation and Freedom* (London, 1964), pp. 7–8, and W. H. Armytage, *A Social History of Engineering* (London, 1969).

15. Harry Braverman (as cited in Note 4), pp. 147–9; Michel Aglietta, *Régulation et Crises du Capitalisme* (Paris, 1976), pp. 97ff.

16. See Benjamin Coriat, *L'Atelier et le Chromomètre* (Paris, 1979), pp. 139ff. It is interesting to note that a "presample" of conveyor-belt production was created by the Chicago meat-packing industry, a clear reflection of the major role played by agriculture in the emergence of American industrialization and American technology, as compared with the British, Belgian, French, German, and Japanese processes.

17. See Karl Marx, *Capital* (Harmondsworth, Middlesex, 1976), Volume 1, Chapter 13/3/C.

18. Aglietta (as cited in Note 15), pp. 143–5; Benjamin Coriat (as cited in Note 16), pp. 227ff; Mario Tronti, *Ouvriers et Capital* (Paris, 1977).

19. See Gareth Stedman Jones, "Class Struggle and the Industrial Revolution," *New Left Review* (1975):35ff.

20. David M. Gordon, "Up and Down the Long Roller Coaster," *U.S. Capitalism in Crisis* (New York, 1978), a series of essays

published by the Union for Radical Political Economics. David M. Gordon, "Stages of Accumulation and Long Economic Cycles," *The Political Economy of the World System* (Beverly Hills, 1980), Volume 3, a series published by Sage.

21. Aglietta drew attention, before Gordon, to the role the transformation of workers' consumer habits played in the emergence of what he called "Fordism" (we would say "late capitalism"). On the same subject, see E. Mandel, *Late Capitalism* (London, 1975), pp. 387–99, and Harry Braverman (as cited in Note 4), Chapter 13. However, Aglietta (like Benjamin Coriat) made the mistake of not relating the increase in real wages made possible by the strong upsurge in the productivity of labor (and the parallel increase in the production of relative surplus value) to the overall tendency of the rate of profit, which is above all a function of the trend of the organic composition of capital. When the rate of profit starts to decline constantly, the further increase in real wages is more and more resisted by capital, its positive effects on the realization of surplus value notwithstanding.

22. Gordon (as cited in the first entry of Note 20), referred to the Japanese Marxist Kozo Uno's "stage theory" of capitalism as a framework for many of his conclusions. We know Uno's work only through the summary of it that appeared in the *Journal of Economic Literature* (1975):853 by Thomas T. Sekine. But in that summary, the mechanical economic-determinist character of the succession of stages comes out much stronger than in Gordon's own writing. According to Sekine, for Uno "the different stages are, therefore, primarily characterized by underlying states of industrial technology which shape conformable industrial and commercial organizations. The latter, at the national level, call forth economic policies (including the denial of any active policies), which lay the ground-work for the deployment of the dominant capital form." In the light of these objections of ours, and of the clearly opposite positions defended, inter alia, in Chapter 5 of *Late Capitalism*, we cannot understand how the "research working group on cyclical rhythms and secular trends" can come to the conclusion that we ignore the importance of political processes (Barr, as cited in Chapter 1, Note 2, p. 490).

23. The French economist Jacques Attali, supposedly the main economic adviser to Socialist Party leader François Mitterrand, recently defended the thesis that "the crisis is already finished," that profits are on the strong upsurge, and that the international

capitalist economy is "restructuring itself" in the Pacific area, at the expense of Western Europe (*Le Monde*, March 1, 1980).

24. Systems Dynamics National Project, annual report 1976, presented to the meeting of corporate sponsors at M.I.T. March 11, 1977; mimeograph D-2715-2, pp 12–13.

25. J. J. Van Duijn, *De Lange Golf in de Economie* (Assen, 1979), pp. 69–74.

26. Jay Forrester, "Business Structure, Economic Cycles and National Policy," *Futures* (1976):205.

Chapter 3

1. Another variable present in this debate is represented by Baran-Sweezy's theory of increasing difficulties of "surplus disposal" under monopoly capitalism, as well as by the different schools defending the theory that contemporary capitalism tends toward permanent stagnation.

2. A recent example: Geoff Hodgson, *Trotsky and Fatalistic Marxism* (London, 1975).

3. One could make out a convincing case that the "orthodox" liberals are not so wrong when they contend that growing state intervention is accompanied by growing waste of economic resources. But the opposite would also be true: Declining state intervention under capitalism would lead to higher and higher levels of underemployment of manpower and equipment, which is likewise a waste of economic resources on a huge scale.

4. Trotsky, together with Varga and other theoreticians of the early years of the Communist International (the main sources for the concept of an "epoch of decline of capitalism"), explicitly stated that a new upsurge in productive forces was possible in spite of that decline, provided that certain social-political conditions were radically altered in favor of capitalism. See Trotsky's report to the Third Congress of the Comintern in 1921 and his critique of the Comintern program of 1928, published, respectively, in *The First Five Years of the Communist International* (New York, 1945), Vol. 1, pp. 174ff, and *The Communist International after Lenin* (New York, 1936), pp. 1ff.

5. On this subject see Marcello De Cecco, *Economia e Finanza internazionale dal 1890 al 1914* (Bari, 1971), and Roger Dehem, *De l'étalon-sterling à l'étalon-dollar* (Paris, 1972). In fact, sterling as reserve currency represented a higher percentage of total central

bank reserves in 1913 than did all other currencies in 1938 (11% as against 7%).

6. The failure of the SDR (supposedly "paper gold") to supplant in any way real gold is not linked only to its avowed purpose, which was to increase, not reduce, "international liquidity." As its creation depends on agreements (i.e., horse deals) between governments, it inevitably reflects these governments' national financial policies (i.e., persistent inflation at nationally varying rates).

7. Folke Hilgert, *The Network of World's Trade* (London, 1940).

8. Significantly enough, this applies to American multinationals too.

9. Percentage annual increases in production per man-hour in manufacturing industry:

	U.S.A.	Japan	GFR	France	Italy	Britain
1960–75	2.7	9.7	5.7	5.6	6.2	3.8
1970–75	1.8	5.4	5.4	3.4	6.0	3.1

U.S. Department of Labor, Bureau of Labor Statistics: "Comparative Growth in Manufacturing Productivity and Labor Costs in Selected Industrialized Countries," Bulletin 1958, 1977, p. 6.

10. The "socialist" countries have just introduced dollar payments in inter-Comecon trade, in the form of fines for excessive ("unplanned") trade imbalance.

11. *Annuaire Statistique des Nations-Unies* (New York, 1977).

12. The World Bank report of 1978 gives the 1976 figure; the 1977 figure is from current OECD and FAO publications; the end-of-1979 figure as well as the end-of-1980 figure are given by a recent OECD publication, summarized in *Le Monde*, August 7, 1980.

13. The average unemployment rate (as percentage of the labor force) was 5.7 percent for the 1870–1913 period in the sixteen OECD countries (Angus Maddison, as cited in Chapter 1, Note 4, p. 115).

14. Let us not forget that even under the so-called conservative management of Arthur F. Burns the Federal Reserve allowed annual rates of increase in the money supply that were between 50 percent and 100 percent superior to the rate of growth of the GNP in real terms.

15. George F. Warren and Frank A. Pearson, *Gold and Prices* (New York, 1935), p. 142.

16. Leon H. Dupriez, "1945 bis 1971 als Aufschwungsphase eines Kondratieff-Zyklus?" *Problèmes économiques contemporains, textes réunis par Paul Löwenthal* (Louvain, 1972), p. 321.

17. Arrighi insisted on the use of inflation "to wipe out the concessions wrested from them [the capitalists] at the point of production by the growing structural strength of the workers." "Towards a Theory of Capitalist Crisis," *New Left Review* (1978):3ff.

18. Michel Aglietta (as cited in Chapter 2, Note 15), pp. 263–9, 297–8, 310–22.

19. The official government sources for these figures are given in Mandel, *The Second Slump* (London, 1978), p. 29. The 1980 projection is based on the rates of growth of consumer and business credit in 1976, 1977, 1978, and 1979.

20. See Mandel, *The Second Slump* (London, 1978), pp. 81–2.

21. *Business Week*, October 16, 1978, April 23, 1979.

22. *Der Spiegel*, February 26, 1979.

23. Our own translation from K. Marx, *Das Kapital* (Berlin, 1969), Volume 3, p. 457 (*Marx-Engels-Werke*, Volume 25).

24. A good anthology of these warnings is provided by von Hayek, *A Tiger by the Tail* (London, 1972). See also Jacques Rueff, *The Monetary Sin of the West* (New York, 1972).

25. An objection is raised against this confirmation of the rising organic composition of capital by some Marxists like Robert Rawthorn. Marx, in *Capital*, Volume 1, and especially in the non-included original "Section VI," stressed the fact that variable capital covers not only wages of manual laborers but also wages of the "collective worker" necessary for the overall production process, including technicians, etc. This is true, and we do not refer in our concept of "labor costs as parts of total production costs" to anything else. But Marx never extended the notion of "collective worker" outside the sphere of production, to include costs of circulation, of commercial wage earners, of state employees, etc., in the concept of "variable capital." He kept the distinction between productive and unproductive labor throughout the four volumes of *Capital*, although with slightly modified frontier lines between them. So he never implied an identity that variable capital equals total national wage bill in the national income.

26. *Le Monde*, October 11, 1978.

27. "Microelectronics: A Survey," *The Economist* 274(1980):4.

28. Harry Braverman (as cited in Chapter 2, Note 4), p. 198. One of the chief German capitalists, Friedrich Bauer from Siemens, quoted by Peter Bartelheimer and Winfried Wolf, "Neue Technologien und BRD/Kapital," *Die Internationale* (1979):42.

29. According to Friedrich Bauer (as cited in Note 28), p. 41, this is only a beginning. Whereas current LSI (large-scale integration) technology makes it possible to pack up to 50,000 "chips" into a single silicon crystal, within three years the number of these chips might climb to 1 million!

30. Bartelheimer and Wolf (as cited in Note 28), pp. 56–9.

31. Bartelheimer and Wolf (as cited in Note 28), p. 54.

32. "Many reasons plead in favor of the idea that for many years, we cannot count any more with a period of long and undisturbed expansion like the one we witnessed during the 25 years preceding 1975. One of these reasons lies among other things in a certain exhaustion of the most profitable technical revolutions which had been 'accumulated' during the thirties and forties, and which after the war leapt towards dominating the development of the economy." Professor Kurt Rothschild, *Wiener Tagebuch*, December 1977.

33. *The Economist*, April 7, 1979.

34. See Christian de Bresson, *L'Innovation selon* Marx (unpublished manuscript).

35. *The Economist* 274(1980):4.

36. "On the other side of the Atlantic, one is more and more conscious of the fact that when innovation develops in the shadow of giant public or private organizations, it not only risks to be oriented towards strengthening acquired positions and rents . . . but that, paradoxically, such an innovation kills innovation." *Le Monde*, December 15, 1978.

37. See W. W. Rostow (as cited in Chapter 1, Note 3), p. 287.

38. A parallel refutation of Rostow's thesis has been offered by Immanuel Wallerstein, "Kondratieff up or Kondratieff down?" *Review* (Binghamton) 2(1979):663ff. Rostow actually goes back to Kondratieff's initial explanation of the long waves [the long-term fluctuations of the terms of trade between industry and agriculture (raw materials)], which the Russian economist himself abandoned rapidly, and which does not stand up against empirical evidence.

39. "It is probable that enough capital plant now exists to sustain output for at least a decade with little additional investment." Jay Forrester, *Fortune* magazine interview, January 16, 1978.

Chapter 4

1. "For the past two decades we have been developing a field called system dynamics using computers to simulate the behavior of complex systems. We found that the interactions between consumer sectors and capital goods sectors can produce a long fluctuation of economic activity spanning 45 to 60 years." Jay Forrester, *Fortune* magazine interview, January 16, 1978.

2. Erik Olin Wright (as cited in Chapter 1, Note 9), pp. 163–4.

3. This is, of course, not to deny the key role that monopoly surplus profits, arising from the capacity of the monopolies to impose "administered" prices in the sectors they dominate, have played in the "permanent inflation" since 1940. But it is the symbiosis of these monopolies with finance capital (i.e., a given credit policy of the banking system) and the servile support the state and the central banks give to that policy that makes the long-term application of these "administered" prices and permanent inflation technically possible.

4. We repeat a quotation from the late Professor Harry Johnson that we previously used in "The Second Slump": "The answer [to inflation] depends . . . in the long run . . . on the will of society to turn away from the Welfare State." *The Banker*, August 1975. Professor Jacques Chevallier stated (*Projet*, March 1980) in an article entitled "The End of the Welfare State" that "on the social field, . . . the effort of solidarity admitted in favor of the poorest layers has to be limited."

5. Robert L. Heilbroner, *Beyond Boom and Crash* (New York, 1978). This psychological explanation of long waves is analogous to the one advanced by the Belgian professor Dupriez and the "generation" explanation advanced by Gerhard Mensch (as cited in Chapter 2, Note 8), p. 74: Grandchildren behave like their grandparents but unlike their parents. This, incidentally, tries to explain the "fifty-year span" of two successive long waves by the age of two successive generations.

6. The French daily *Le Monde*, in spite of its semiofficial status, has become scared by the penetration into official circles of the Giscardist government party of the ideologues of the GRECE group

(Groupement de Recherches et d'Etudes pour la Civilisation européenne), who openly defend a series of classic themes of the fascist (or neofascist) extreme right: anti-egalitarianism, hostility toward the "liberal" state, rejection not only of Marxism but also of the "oriental Judeo-Christian tradition," etc. For a good study of the GRECE and all its implications, see *The New York Review of Books*, January 24, 1980, Thomas Sheehan, *Paris: Moses and Polytheism*, pp. 13f.

7. A rather terrifying manifestation of the growth of this antihumanitarian and life-despising trend in popular "subculture" was the tremendous success (millions of readers and millions of spectators throughout the capitalist world) of the book and movie *Damien*, whose central theme, reduced to its final "message," is an exhortation to kill a young boy because he is the "reincarnation of Satan," who, if he stays alive, will bring misery and death to many people. Carl Sagan, in "The Paradoxers," *Broca's Brain* (New York, 1978), has likewise rightly denounced the wave of pseudoscience and antiscience now flooding America, under the cover of protestant fundamentalist revivalism, such as *The Late Great Planet Earth* (New York, 1975) (10 million copies sold) and books ridiculing evolution.

8. As a later study of the Club of Rome admitted, once one accepts the hypothesis that there are no limits to the advance of human science, inventive ingenuity, and capacity to adapt social institutions to the survival needs of the species, the conclusions of "Limits of Growth" fall.

9. We have deliberately divided the 1893–1940 span into two separate periods to stress the historical importance of the watershed of 1914–18 (i.e., the beginning of the epoch of decline of capitalism and decomposition of the capitalist world system). Hans Rosenberg's book on the "long depression 1872–1893" is an impressive example of treating a long wave as a specifically structured historical period (as cited in Chapter 1, Note 2).

10. We use this term in analogy with the function Marx attributed to crises of overproduction during the normal business cycle.

11. A detailed description of many new techniques made possible by microprocessing in nearly all areas of social life, from production to banking to teaching to administration, is provided by Dieter Balkhausen, *Die dritte industrielle Revolution* (Dusseldorf, 1978). On the possibilities (and dangers) of genetic engineering techniques,

see *The Economist* 273(1980):53 and *Le Monde*, February 6, 1980, p. 17

12. Ibid., pp. 100ff; Bartelheimer and Wolf (as cited in Chapter 3, Note 28), pp. 47–9.

13. *Ventil* (1979):11.

14. *Deutsche Zeitung/Christ und Welt*, September 8, 1978.

15. Bartelheimer and Wolf (as cited in Chapter 3, Note 28), p. 49.

16. Mr Jean Vogé (*Le Monde*, February 24, 1980, p. XIII) relates this problem to a supposed "galloping inflation of information expenditure necessary to the organisation of the socio-economic system." More practically, we would rather note that it is due to a time lag between mass-scale production of consumer goods in general and mass-scale production of that type of "new" consumer goods that could replace services based on individualized human labor.

17. *The Times*, November 23, 1978.

18. See the statements made by ITT representatives at a conference in Geneva, November 9–10, 1978, organized by, among other institutions, the International Chamber of Commerce (*Le Monde*, November 12–13, 1978). Regarding the controversy about unemployment in Britain, see Clive Jenkins and Barrie Sherman, *The Collapse of Work* (London, 1979), and *The Economist*, June 9, 1979.

19. See the interesting debate between the leader of the German trade unions, Vetter, and the late Mr Schleyer, chairman of the West German employers' federation, in which the former insisted on the "right to work" (i.e., full employment), the latter on the "duty to work" (i.e., the need for the workers to work harder and expect less from social security under conditions of massive unemployment) (*Neue Zürcher Zeitung* May 25, 1977). One does not need any "conspiracy theory" to understand that under late capitalism (all the humbug of the "mixed economy" and the "welfare state" notwithstanding), the objective function of the massive unemployment condoned by *all* Western governments is precisely to impose that "more responsible" attitude on the workers (i.e., to "discipline" them into increasing the production of absolute surplus value, as Marxists would say).

20. One seemingly more palatable variant of such an attempt to drive up the rate of profit, without going to the extreme of completely destroying all democratic freedoms, would appear to be the

form of statutory income policies for which left Keynesians like Professor Galbraith increasingly campaign. The growing call in favor of more imperative planning (which unites such different figures in the United States as the liberal professor Heilbroner and the New York investment banker Felix Rohatyn) apparently points in the same direction. However, a moment's thought will indicate that such a stopgap intermediate solution would only postpone the moment of reckoning (as did the "golden years" of the Weimar Republic in the 1920s) without in any way avoiding it. A militant, well-organized, and at the same time beleaguered working class will not voluntarily accept a long-term de facto freeze or even decline in real wages, even under "friendly left" governments. This the British and West German employers found out to their dismay during the year 1978, as did the reformist leaders of those countries. So the question remains: How can this militancy and resistance of the workers be decisively broken, without violent curtailment of the right to strike, which implies no less heavy infringement on freedom of the press, the right of association and demonstration, etc.?

21. W. W. Rostow (as cited in Chapter 1, Note 3), p. 630.

22. See an excellent comment on that report by Samuel Bowles, "The Trilateral Commission: Have Capitalism and Democracy Come to a Parting of the Ways?" *U.S. Capitalism in Crisis* (as cited in Chapter 2, Note 20), pp. 261ff.

23. Some of the truly horrifying aspects of the Southern Hemisphere's misery, in spite of (or should one say often in function of) "development progress," are revealed in health studies. According to the World Health Organization report presented at a London conference, June 5–6, 1978, three-quarters of mankind (3.2 billion human beings of the 4 billion inhabitants of our planet) have no access whatsoever to medical aid. Of the 80 million children who are born every year in so-called third-world countries. 5 million die and 10 million remain seriously handicapped as a result of illnesses incurred during the first period of life (*Le Monde*, June 8, 1978). Fifty-five percent of the inhabitants of these countries (i.e., more than 1 billion human beings) suffer from malnutrition, but this goes up to 62.8 percent for children, and it seriously impairs the development of their intellectual capacities. S. Reutlinger and M. Selowsky, "Malnutrition and Poverty," World Bank occasional paper No. 23, 1976. J. Cravieto and E. de Licardie, "The Effect of Malnutrition on the Individual," A. Berg et al., eds., *Nutrition,*

National Development and Planning (Cambridge, Mass., 1973).

24. As a matter of fact, the big "success stories" in industrialization of third-world countries during the 1960s and 1970s, such as the Brazilian and South Korean stories, were made possible by a radical reduction, not an increase, in real wages, thereby implying that the "internal market" did not go beyond the middle classes. *The New York Times* (July 28, 1979) published a sober estimate by Sylvia Ann Hewlett of the "costs of growth" in the semicolonial countries: "Capitalist strategies, for example, in Nigeria, the Philippines and Brazil, have achieved rapid rates of economic growth, but such economic dynamism has rested on mass misery. In these countries, at least half of the citizenry has been excluded from the modernization process and remains in abject poverty." The proportion indicated is much below reality, in our opinion.

25. The most striking example is provided by the textile industry, for which the annual rate of growth in total demand (whether served by native goods or by imported goods) is down to 2 percent in the OECD countries.

26. OCDE: "L'incidence des nouveaux pays industriels sur la production et les échanges des produits manufacturés," Paris, June 1979.

27. In 1976, the so-called socialist countries purchased 2.5 percent of American expons, 5.5 percent of EEC exports, and 6 percent of Japanese exports, and they achieved this modest result only by piling up large debts.

28. According to the *Financial Times*, July 6, 1979, "the Third World was largely self-sufficient in food grains up to 1950 but net grain imports reached 50 million tonnes in 1975 and are expected to reach 100 million tonnes during the 1980s." Robin Sokal gives the figure of third-world grain deficits at 85 million tonnes in 1979 and 145 million tonnes in 1980 (*La Stampa*, June 25, 1980).

29. Schumpeter used the term "creative destruction" as a description of the process by which technologically backward firms are ruthlessly eliminated by "innovating" firms under capitalism. It is the title of Chapter 7 of *Capitalism, Socialism and Democracy*, 3rd ed. (New York, 1962).

30. An example of such ideological preparation and "ideal" anticipation is provided by the "science fiction" book *The Third World War: August 1985*, written not by a professional novelist but by General Sir John Hacket and other top-ranking NATO

generals and advisors. The function of the book is obviously to prepare the climate not only for a new upsurge in armament
expenditure but also for eventual preventive military action by imperialism against "threatening Soviet aggression." What value is left to
such ideological assertions in the 1990s?

Chapter 5

1. Immanuel Wallerstein, "Long Waves as Capitalist Process,"
paper submitted to the Colloquium *Research on Long Waves*, Paris,
March 17–19, 1993. Wallerstein bases himself on, among others,
Braudel and Spooner, "Prices in Europe 1450 to 1750," in
Cambridge Economic History of Europe, Vol. 4.

2. I. Wallerstein, "A Brief Agenda for the Future of Long-Wave
Research," in Kleinknecht, Mandel, and Wallerstein, eds., *New
Findings in Long Wave Research* (London, 1992).

3. Solomos Solomou, *Phases of Economic Growth 1850–1973*
(Cambridge, 1987).

4. Ibid., p. 56.

5. Solomou disregards the fact that a large number of economic
historians clearly identify long waves prior to 1872: at least the
long depression of 1826–48 and the long expansion of 1848–73.

6. Solomou (as cited in Note 3), pp. 161f., 171.

7. Alfred Kleinknecht, *Innovation Patterns in Crisis and
Prosperity* (London, 1987), pp. 23–4.

8. Christopher Freeman, ed., *Long Waves in the World Economy*
(London, 1983).

9. Andrew Tylecote, *The Long Wave in the World Economy*
(London, 1992), p. 18.

10. Jesús Albarracín, *La onda larga del capitalismo español*
Collegio de Economistas de Madrid, 1987; and see the work of
Fontvielle for France; Glismann, Rodemer and Wolter for Germany;
Antonio Piaseo for Belgium; and the Kiel Institute for World
Economics for a number of countries.

11. Paul Boccara et al., "Cycles longs, mutations et crise," *Issues*
16(1983); and "Cycles longs et la longue phase de difficultés,"
Issues 29(1987).

12. See the German translation, Stanislaw Menschikow, *Lange
Wellen in der Wirtschaft* (Frankfurt/Main, 1989).

13. Ibid., p. 102.

14. John Sterman, "The Economic Long Wave: Theory and

Evidence," in T. Vasko, ed., *The Long Wave Debate* (Berlin, 1987).

15. Anwar Shaikh, in *New Findings* (as cited in Note 2), p. 175.

16. Ibid., p. 185.

17. Rabah Benakouche, *Inflacão e Crise* (Persepolis, 1981), pp. 95–6.

18. Duménil and Lévy, *The Economics of the Profit Rate* (Brookfield, 1993), p. 274.

19. Ibid., p. 251.

20. See Mahdavi, *Technological Innovation, an Efficiency Investigation* (Stockholm, 1972).

21. Freeman (as cited in Note 8), Chapter 6.

22. Kleinknecht (as cited in Note 7).

23. Mensch, Coutinho, and Kaasch, Chapter 4 in Freeman, ed. (as cited in Note 8).

24. Anwar Shaikh has written what seems to be the definitive study of capacity utilization in the United States.

25. In November 1993 an international rally of electric cars took place in the French city of La Rochelle.

26. Sharp cuts in state subsidies to the health sector have forced drug companies to curtail their R & D expenditure. *Financial Times*, March 23, 1994.

27. Christopher Freeman, "The Third Kondratieff Wave," paper submitted to the symposium on long waves held in Brussels in January 1989.

28. The dramatic decline in real wages in Latin America is reflected in the following figures:

Industrial wages in real terms

	1980	1988–89	1990–91	1992–93
Argentina	100.0	90.1	79.9	77.5
Brazil	100.0	78.7	88.0	97.3
Chile	100.0	101.3	106.7	114.2
Colombia	100.0	122.3	130.9	134.5
Mexico	100.0	61.1	65.8	71.0
Peru	100.0	60.2	37.9	39.6
Venezuela	100.0	48.0	40.2	40.6

Source: IDB (1993), ECLA (1993), World Bank (2)

29. In *New Findings* (as cited in Note 2), p. 331.

Andre Gunder Frank contends that our thesis on the relative autonomy of class-struggle outcomes from the prevailing economic conditions is somehow related to our political commitment to world revolution, i.e. to the offensive potential of the working class. An examination of what I stated at the Brussels Symposium, at which Gunder Frank was present, and what I say in this book, will show that this is not at all the case.

I stress the defensive nature of the workers' struggles against capital's attempts, since the onset of the long depressive wave, as well as the fact that failure or success of these struggles is not economically predetermined.

In other words, I stress the dialectic of the objective and subjective factors in history, and the need to oppose parametrical to mechanical determinism.

Chapter 6

1. David Gordon, "Stages of Accumulation and Long Economic Crisis," mimeographed, p. 38, later to appear in Hopkins and Wallerstein, eds., *Processes in the World System* (London, 1980).

2. "Aggregate Demand and Kondratieff Cycle: A Methodological Note," *Newsletter on Long Waves*, sponsored by the Fernand Braudel Center and the Maison des Sciences de l'Homme, Paris, April 1987.

3. "Wages, Price and Profit," in *Marx-Engels Selected Works* (Moscow, 1968), p. 223.

4. *Grundrisse* (Harmondsworth, Middlesex, 1975), pp. 287–8.

5. Pascal Buléon of the University of Caen has written a convincing analysis of what he calls "an international cycle of labor conflicts" in the 1970s and 1980s in Europe.

6. Francisco Louça, "A Transição de 'Paradigma tecno-económico' como factor das ondas do desenvolvimiento capitalista: o caso da revolução micro-eletrónica," masters' dissertation, Lisbon, June 1993, p. 113.

7. In addition to Kuhn's well-known book *The Structure of Scientific Revolutions*, Louça mentions Bonaventura Santos, *Introdução a uma Ciencia Posmoderna* (Oporto, 1989), and René Thom, "Les limites nécessaires de l'investigation scientifique," mimeographed communication to the colloquium organized by the

Franco-Portuguese Institute, Lisbon, 1993. These sources should be added to those we cite in Chapter 2.

8. In the mean time, Louçã has written a new book (*Turbulence in Economics: the long historical perspective of the long waves of capitalist development*) that, by its bibliography, the richness and diversity of its analysis, the extensive use of mathematical methods of verification and proof, is by far the best book up till now on the long waves problematic. It is quite superior to my own work. However, precisely because of its extreme sophistication and its length, it is probably not accessible to all those interested in the long waves discussion. It is also less clear in its conclusions than this book.

François Chesnais (*La Mondialisation du capital*, Syros, Paris, 1994) correctly establishes the correlation between the so-called "globalization" phenomenon, the predominance of the multinational corporations, and the tremendous expansion of financial operations. But, contrary to our analysis, he does not give weight to the relative autonomy of the class-struggle waves and their possible outcomes.

9. The same is true of the rhythm of destruction of the "old middle classes" (independent peasants, tradespeople, handicraftsmen, etc.), as well as general population trends.

10. Lydia Potts, *Weltmarkt für Arbeitskraft* (Hamburg, 1988), especially pp. 164–90.

11. More recently there has been large-scale migration from a number of countries to the sparsely populated oil-exporting Arab states.

12. The chief exception is the flow into the so-called "empty countries" before the American Civil War, which was in any case minor in comparison with what happened later. It should be added that these countries were simultaneously being "emptied" of their original inhabitants.

13. In a commodity-producing society, labor power is not simply a commodity. It is a commodity attached to human beings, who can react (at least up to a point) to what the market tries to impose on them. A ton of steel or a bundle of chips is not capable of such reactions.

14. See his report to the symposium held in March 1933 in Marilla, Brazil.

15. Eric Tucker, p. 49 of a mimeographed text published by the Center for Research on Work and Society, York University, Canada.

16. *New Findings* (as cited in Chapter 5, Note 2), pp. 286–93. We leave aside the question of whether this way of assessing the vicissitudes of class struggle is really adequate. We rather doubt it.

17. Giorgio Gattei, "Every Twenty-Five Years: Strike Waves and Long Economic Cycles," p. 15.

18. Ernesto Screpanti, "Long Cycles in Strike Activity, an Empirical Investigation," *British Journal of Industrial Relations* (March 1987).

19. Ernesto Screpanti, "Long Economic Cycles and Recurring Proletarian Insurgency," *Review* (Research Foundation of SUNY) VII/3 (Winter 1984).

20. The present scale of inflation, of the debt economy, is quite staggering. Dollar debts (i.e., excluding those denominated in other currencies) have reached the figure of $10 trillion: $10,000,000,000,000, of which, incidentally, only 15 percent represents the dollar debt of so-called third-world countries – which after all represents 50 percent of humanity. Michael Moffitt's book *The World's Money: International Banking from Bretton Woods to the Brink of Insolvency* (New York, 1983) offers an interesting analysis of the origins and development of the "debt economy."

21. Nikolai Bukharin, "Imperialism and the Accumulation of Capital," in Rosa Luxemburg and Nikolai Bukharin, *Imperialism and the Accumulation of Capital*, ed. K. Tarbuck (London, 1972), pp. 256–7.

22. Gilbert Achcar's PhD entitled "L'Empire et l'argent – Essai sur les fondements de la stratégie impériale des Etats-Unis" offers a very thorough and sophisticated analysis of the use of foreign policy by the US ruling class – which Achcar defines in a more subtle and precise way than is generally the case – to counterbalance the relative decline of the US's economic and financial hegemony in the world.

23. Predominant does not mean exclusive. Surviving alongside the multinationals are "national" monopolies, corporations with state participation, nationalized corporations, as well as small and medium-sized enterprises operating essentially in the home market.

24. For some years now the "Bank of International Settlements" in Basle, wrongly considered as the "central bank of central banks," has admitted in its annual reports that the exact amount of "floating capital" is not known at all. Estimates differ by hundreds of billions of dollars.

NOTES

25. As long as private property exists, paper money issued by private bankers can always be used to gain private profits (advantages) at the expense of other owners of capital.

26. Samir Amin (*Monthly Review*, October 1993) makes the point that as a result of the qualitative increase in "globalization" of the world economy (internationalization of the productive forces), "world capitalism needs a world organization on all levels, on the monetary level certainly, but also on the political level. It needs a 'world central bank', and therefore a new world money issued by the bank, or if not, it needs a world state . . ." We would replace the words "if not" with "and therefore." No real "world central bank" is possible without a world state. And for reasons made clear in the text and in footnote 20, such a world state is a will-o'-the-wisp as long as the major means of production and exchange continue to be privately owned.

27. All data from "La révolution microélectronique," in *Pour la Science 1979*, based on articles from the *Scientific American* (1977).

28. Robert Noyce (*Scientific American*, 1977) points out that stepped-up expenditure for research could more than offset these losses. But the cheaper the new integrated circuits and the chips, the greater the output that has to be sold to maintain profits. This proved impossible. Hence, the crisis of profitability which hit first the American, then the European and Japanese semi-conductor and microchip producers.

Fritz Halbach (*Kapitalismus ohne Krisen?*, Prolit-Verlag, Giessen, 1972) has written a coherent, be it only theoretical and not empirically founded, defense of the tendencial law of decline of the average rate of profit.

29. This is a straight quote from Daniel Bell, "Downfall of the Business Giants," *Dissent* (Summer 1993). But the title, and the conclusion, are certainly premature and suffer from excessive extrapolation.

30. *Financial Times*, September 10, 1993.

31. Starting from the same sectorial examples in France, Italy, and Japan, Christian Palloix (*Les Firmes multinationales et le procès d'internationalisation*, Paris, Maspéro, 1973) had tried to relate the internationalization of the productive forces and the operations of the multinational corporations to the logic of capital as analysed by Marx.

32. *Financial Times*, September 10, 1993.

163

33. A confused and confusing discussion has taken place of late on the future of employment in the wake of the explosion of the so-called information technology (IT) sector. Optimists expressing themselves in, for example, *The Economist* (February 11, 1995) register a big increase in jobs like home-health workers, computer systems analysts and programmers, travel agents, childcare workers, guards, restaurant cooks, nurses, gardeners, janitor, and cleaners, doctors and lawyers. Whether this increase could offset the steep decline in jobs in the traditional service industries provoked by IT – indeed this is the main consequence of IT! – is more than dubious.

On these conflicting data and views see, among others, "The OECD Jobs Study: Evidence and Explanations"; Paul Krugman, "Past and Perspective Causes of High Unemployment" (Economic Symposium of the Federal Reserve Bank of Kansas City at Jackson Hole, August 1994).

34. In *OMNI*, New York (April 1983).

35. General Motors invested $80 billion in the 1980s to introduce full automation of the giant Hamtrack plant in Detroit. But "what was meant to be a showcase plant turned into a nightmare." See "GM's Robots Run Amok," *The Economist*, August 10, 1991. The "human factor" proved decisive.

36. According to *Scientific American* (February 1995), engineers have developed a memory chip that can hold a billion bits of information and a microprocessor that performs in excess of a billion instructions per second, a thousand-fold increase in capacity and processing power since the 1980s.

The price (the article does not specify whether it is cost price or sales price) will have gone down from $10 in the 1950s to a hundred thousandth of a cent a few years from now. But manufacturing and especially sales questions are far from being solved.

Index

abstract science 30
Acona University 117
Africa 87, 123
aggregate demand 90–91, 117
Aglietta, Michel 61
Albarracín, Jesús 103
Alessandri regime 94
Althusser, Louis 38
Altvater, Elmar 6, 124–5
Amdahl (company) 67
annual compound rate of growth
  3, 5
anti-humanist values 82, 94
applied science 30, 120
Argentina 56, 103
arms industry/trade 18, 53–4, 56,
  59, 94, 95, 131
Asia 87, 131
Asia-dollar markets 55
assembly-line production 33–6
  passim
Auschwitz 93
austerity policies 78, 87
autarky 104
automation
  machine systems 33, 34–5, 112
  semiautomation 33, 64–7, 84–6,
  136
autonomy, relative 6, 37, 38,
  40–42, 114, 115, 120, 129

balance of payments 52, 54, 55–6
bank credit 27, 58, 61
Bank of England 51
Bank of International Settlements
  162 (n24)
bank money inflation 61

banks 51–2, 53, 61, 137
barbarism 42, 94
Bebel, A. 118
Belgium 6, 103
Benakouche, Rabah 109
Bernal, J.D. 29
Boccara, Paul 104, 105
bourgeois culture 94, 95
bourgeois ideology 36, 80, 81
bourgeois society 30, 31, 51, 105,
  118
bourgeois states 52, 131–2
bourgeoisie 20, 34, 129, 131
Braudel, Fernand 116
Braverman, Harry 29
Brazil 90
breakdown theory controversy 9
Bretton Woods system 25, 53,
  75
Britain 15, 98, 102, 125
  capital-labor relations 87, 133
  capital expenditure 135
  General Strike 126
  growth rate 2, 3, 6, 21–2
  imperialism 23–4, 25, 51, 63,
  131
  pound sterling 51, 53, 56, 59
  world hegemony 56
Brussels symposium (1989) 116,
  126
Bukharin, Nikolai 131
Burroughs (company) 67
business cycle 107, 114, 117–18
  in long wave theory 4, 8, 11, 12,
  21–2, 97, 99, 105
  patent cycle and 31–2
Business Week 62

165

liquidity crisis 13
"long-maturing investment projects" 19
"long-term cycle" 22
long cycle hypothesis 104, 126–7
long waves
  inflation and (end of postwar boom) 49–75
  international debate 97–115
  new issues/clarifications 116–38
  technical revolutions and (class struggle cycles) 28–48
  as specific historical periods 76–96
long waves theory
  application of (current situation) 6, 91–6
  application of (pre-1826) 5–6
  average rate of profit 7, 8, 9–21
  gold production 25–7
  industrial cycle and 21–3
  international capitalist competition 23–5
  key indicators of Marxist theory 6–11
  statistical data 1–5
Louça, Francisco 120
Luxemburg, Rosa 118

M.I.T. 43, 74, 106–7
McCarthyism 18
machine systems 33, 34–5, 112
Maclaurin, W. Rupert 32
Maddison, Angus 2, 5
Maison des Sciences de l'Homme 116
Malaysia 55
Malthus, Thomas 10, 117
Mandel, Ernest 2, 18, 28, 29, 61, 65, 107, 108
manufactured goods 54, 55, 66, 70
Marshall Plan 7, 25, 106
Marx, Karl 6–11 *passim*, 17, 19, 22–3, 27–9, 35, 60, 64, 95, 98, 106–8, 115, 117–21, 135, 136
Marxists 80–81, 97, 102, 105, 114, 117
  class struggle and 30, 38, 40

inflation and 49–50, 53, 60–61, 63, 65
key indicators of long waves theory 6–11
long waves theory 1, 6–11, 13, 15–16, 21–3, 26, 76, 107–8
revolutionary 49–50, 92–3
mass production 35, 66, 68
material goods 81
material production 63
mechanistic-economic determinism 42, 115
Mensch, Gerhard 30, 32, 110–11
Menshikov, Stanislav 104, 105–6
Mexico 90, 100, 122
microprocessors 67, 84, 85, 86, 91
migration 20–21, 121–4, 125
militancy 36–8, 83, 88, 117, 118, 126–8
military power 24, 25, 56, 130
monetarism 57, 77, 78
monetary crisis 13
monetary policy 62
money
  capital 7, 8, 13, 19
  movements 6
  privatization of 131, 134
  quantity theory 26, 54, 61
  "world money" 51–2, 53, 134
monopolistic rents 110
monopoly capital 88
monopoly capitalism 149 (n1)
Montpellier University 116
multinational corporations 41, 75, 84, 131
multiplier 117
Mussolini, Benito 89
mysticism 79–80

Napoleonic Wars 6, 82
national economies 100, 103
national liberation movements 25, 40, 70, 90, 92, 114
natural sciences 79, 80
neo-reformism 137
Nigeria 90
nonagricultural private firms (Japan) 13, 14